John Rhey Thompson

Christian Manliness

And other Sermons

John Rhey Thompson

Christian Manliness
And other Sermons

ISBN/EAN: 9783743353886

Manufactured in Europe, USA, Canada, Australia, Japa

Cover: Foto ©Lupo / pixelio.de

Manufactured and distributed by brebook publishing software (www.brebook.com)

John Rhey Thompson

Christian Manliness

CHRISTIAN MANLINESS,

AND

OTHER SERMONS.

BY

JOHN RHEY THOMPSON D.D.

OF THE NEW YORK CONFERENCE

NEW YORK: HUNT & EATON
CINCINNATI: CRANSTON & STOWE
1889

Copyright, 1889, by
HUNT & EATON,
NEW YORK.

This Book

IS RESPECTFULLY DEDICATED

TO MY KIND AND GENEROUS FRIEND,

MR. JOHN D. SLAYBACK,

OF NEW YORK,

WHO SO BEAUTIFULLY ILLUSTRATES IN HIS LIFE AND

CHARACTER THE CHRISTIAN MANLINESS

I SEEK HEREIN TO COMMEND.

CONTENTS.

	PAGE
CHRISTIAN MANLINESS—WHAT IS IT?	1
CHRISTIAN MANLINESS—AS TESTED BY POVERTY	17
CHRISTIAN MANLINESS—AS PUT TO THE PROOF IN PUBLIC LIFE	36
JESUS AND THE GREAT MASTERS OF LITERATURE	53
GREAT MEN IN HISTORY	68
CHRISTIAN MANLINESS IN TRIAL	85
THE SPIRITUAL PROPHECIES OF CHRISTIAN MANLINESS	98
THE DESIRE FOR DEATH	113
THE IDENTIFICATION OF DIVINITY WITH HUMANITY	125
MODERN PROGRESS AN ENCOURAGEMENT TO MISSIONARY ZEAL	135
THE GREAT KING IN DISGUISE	149
THE PROPHETIC VISION OF GOD	158
THE BRAVE CHOICE OF MOSES	173
SIGNIFICANT OMISSIONS IN THE PREACHING OF JESUS	187
THE MORAL HARVEST	199
THE GREATNESS OF JESUS	214
THE CALL OF ABRAHAM	233
LAW IN THE SPIRITUAL REALM	243
THE REASONABLENESS OF IMMORTALITY—I	260
THE REASONABLENESS OF IMMORTALITY—II	276
THE CHRISTIAN HEAVEN	289

CHRISTIAN MANLINESS—WHAT IS IT?

> Pilate therefore said unto him, Art thou a king then? Jesus answered, Thou sayest that I am a king. To this end was I born, and for this cause came I into the world, that I should bear witness unto the truth. Every one that is of the truth heareth my voice.—John xviii, 37.

IN the historical drama of "Julius Cæsar" the two principal characters among the conspirators are Cassius and Brutus. After the sudden and irreparable overthrow of their perilous fortunes on the fatal field of Philippi, they both took their own lives. It is not over the dead body of the designing and envious Cassius, however, but over that of the noble and patriotic, albeit misguided, Brutus, that Marc Antony speaks the well-known lines:

> "This was the noblest Roman of them all:
> All the conspirators save only he
> Did that they did in envy of great Cæsar;
> He only in a general honest thought
> And common good to all made one of them.
> His life was gentle, and the elements
> So mixed in him that Nature might stand up
> And say to all the world, 'THIS WAS A MAN.'"

Our great Shakespeare here finely describes the elements of the manhood of Brutus. He was true, patriotic, unselfish, magnanimous, gentle—of such rare and admirable equipoise that Nature might stand up and say to all the world, " This was a man." The outside, apparent, physical, palpable victory is with Marc Antony; the real, inside, invisible, moral victory is with Brutus. Flushed with success, soon to become the master of the whole world, Antony is constrained to step aside and pay high tribute to the glorious virtues of his dead foe. One had better be Brutus, dead yonder on the Philippian plain, than Marc Antony, alive in the arms of Cleopatra! Death, with one's honor and purity untarnished, is better than life stained with dishonor and corrupted by lust—this is the lesson of history, of conscience, of philosophy, of religion.

In what consists manliness? That manliness, I mean, which enables its possessors to become rulers, masters, disposers of the circumstances, limitations, conditions, forces, fates of human life. It is clear that it is not in any thing obese, gross, or sensual, in any thing purely physical or animal; it does not reside in bodily strength or agility or endurance. When Nelson was a boy fourteen years of age he attacked a polar bear with a handspike, and when he was reproved for it by his captain he simply stated that he had never made the acquaintance of Mr. Fear. He was a mere shadow of a man ; he could not have stood before the Boston "slugger," Sullivan, two minutes, but in the Bay of Aboukir and at Trafalgar, under the solemn inspiration of duty, one Nelson was worth a million Sullivans. The prize-fighters, the athletes, the victors in the Grecian games, the men who won the famous laurel-leaf crowns, the rowers, the wrestlers, all the men who have come to power and conspicuity by the force of mere flesh or muscle or nerve—when have they ever rekindled the extinguished torches of human progress? When have they carried out into the unknown darkness the new light? When have they been the helpers of their brother-men? When have they stood in the solitary outposts of liberty to herald the coming of the better days? When have they refined, elevated, enriched civilization? When have they controlled destinies? Yonder is the great, the gifted, and the brilliant Alcibiades, fortunate in his birth, in his family, in his training, in his beauty, in his grace, in his eloquence, and come, too, at a time when Greece needs a great man; but he is gross, false, sensual, fickle, corrupt, and he but precipitates the ruin of the land he might have saved. On the other hand, there is Baxter, of Kidderminster, whose life, as it is described by one of his biographers, was one continual struggle with disease, and he goes into the most degraded and heathenish parish in all England, where church-going was the exception and brutal prize-fighting was the rule, and in a few years the conditions were precisely reversed. And there is William of Orange, the slight, pale, feeble, wheezing, asthmatic invalid, with all the contending factions of English politics about him, with the great diplomatists of the continent of Europe eagerly planning his overthrow; but he holds on to life with an eager and tenacious grasp, and finally forms the mighty coalition that broke the power and humbled the pride of the Grand Monarque.

Nor is Christian manliness, as here conceived, to be mistaken for the brilliant qualities, the high executive energy, of the great soldiers of the world. If so, then Alexander, petulant, cruel, selfish, intemperate, lustful, was a manly man; then the first Duke of Marlborough, corroded by avarice, the slave of passion, the tool of every master, was a manly man; then Napoleon, cold, pitiless, remorseless, with an utterly unscrupulous and remorseless ambition, was a manly man.

Our manliness is to be distinguished from mere talents or taste or scholarship. Erasmus had taste, talents, scholarship; he was a good judge of a fine picture; he was the best Greek scholar of his time; he could have edited the most perfect copy of the New Testament; he loved brilliant society; but it took a man made of sterner stuff to defy the seemingly omnipresent and irresistible power of the papacy. It took a plain, sturdy, rugged man, like Martin Luther, who knew indeed less about Greek, but a great deal more about God.

Success is not manliness. Robert Walpole was successful in governing England for many years, but he did it by knowing the price of each purchasable member of Parliament. He ruled England for a generation, but his letters and the history of the period reveal that the secret of his rule is to be found in his unerring discernment of the exact number of pounds sterling required to give him a majority. Greatness of character is not to be confounded with intellectual acuteness, penetration, or vigor. One may be the founder of a new, benevolent, and world-revolutionizing system of philosophy and yet be deficient in manhood. Bacon, delaying the trial of causes and turning an itching palm to wealthy suitors, eager for the bribe, is not a picture of a manly man. He was, indeed, the " greatest, the wisest, and the *meanest* of mankind!"

Nor is genius, however splendid, a substitute for manhood. The world owes more to its plain, sturdy, plodding, duty-loving John Howards, Samuel Wilberforces, George Peabodys, and Henry Wilsons than to all its fierce, fitful, lurid Byrons and Poes. The critics may be right when they say that Shelley had naturally larger, finer, richer poetic powers than our Longfellow, but while the fame of Shelley is narrowing, dwarfing, and dying, our poet has entered on a fresh, green, wide, lasting fame.

Manhood is not to be confounded with mere passivity of moral disposition. The goodness which is so often recommended to us, dry, jejune, tasteless, insipid, without aggression, without force, without spontaneity, without inspiration, deficient in courage, in electric force and contagiousness, is not the goodness which graces and crowns a strong and noble manhood. I love to read about the seraphic Summerfield. Doubtless his conversation was in heaven; but, as I read the history, I am reminded that it took the steady, sagacious, persistent, iron-willed Francis Asbury to found in the wilds of this New World that Methodism which should ultimately become the dominant faith of the American people. Fletcher of Madeley was indeed saintly; he, if any man, might honestly use the words of the Psalmist, and say, "Whom have I in heaven but thee? and whom do I desire on earth besides thee?" But England in the last century required a type of piety more rugged, more robust, more aggressive, and, if I may say it without misconstruction, a trifle more secular—the kind of piety embodied in the life and work of John Wesley. Philip Melanchthon was gentle and sweet-spirited, but I have always doubted whether he would have publicly burned the pope's bull, rejected the cardinal's hat, and have stood alone in the Diet of Worms and defied all the forces of the empire.

Christian manliness means something more than to be complacent and amiable; something more than to keep ourselves scrupulously clean from the defiling touch of evil. This manliness carries with it the willingness to declare the truth, to defend the right, to suffer and to die, if need be, for the right. Three words, if they do not entirely describe, are distinctly included in, the Christian idea of manliness: courage, dutifulness, love. Neither of these words alone would give an adequate conception of the ideal manliness. Courage alone will not, for courage may be, and doubtless often is, the result simply of physical conditions, of abounding animal spirits. Dutifulness alone will not, for dutifulness may be hard, ungracious, rigid, constrained, and not bright, open, genial, spontaneous in expression. Love alone will not, for, unless tied fast to a supreme sense of duty and made willing to face with fortitude pain, sacrifice, difficulties, and death, there is danger that love will evaporate in mere sentiment. The pilot of the Mississippi steamboat had Christian manliness when, discovering the boat to be on fire, and calculating the distance to the shore, he stood at the wheel until he beached her, and then fell a blackened corpse. He had the three qualities; courage, dutifulness, love. He was no scholar, no genius: he did not know the parts of speech; he could not have told the difference between a verb and a noun; his usual manner of expressing himself was slangy; he would have had an uncomfortable time in a Fifth Avenue parlor—his feet and hands would have been very much in the way, his face would have been red and fiery—but in the darkness of the solemn night, as the fierce breath of the flames drew ever nearer, the voice of the Eternal was heard by him, and he nobly laid down his life a sacrifice for others. Twelve or thirteen years ago, on the coast of Scotland, seven boys went out to fish in a small boat, when, going suddenly to one side, it upset, and they found themselves struggling with the waves. The oldest boy, thirteen years of age, Alexander Sutherland, alone knew how to swim, and one after another he landed five of his companions, and, returning for the sixth, he became exhausted and sank in the waves. Here is courage, dutifulness, love.

> "He dares and sinks and dies alone,
> With all the saved in view;
> A Christ among the fisher lads,
> The ransom of his crew."

You have heard of the wreck of the *Birkenhead*. The very highest Christian manliness was found in the men who constituted the passengers of that ship. The sea below them was full of sharks; there were enough boats to land the women and the children. Captain Wright knew, and the men knew, that the ship could not float until the boats came back, and he ordered them on deck in companies, and told them to stand at "attention;" and there they stood, never uttering a word, until the ship keeled over and they all went down. That was manliness—courage, dutifulness, love.

The very soul of manhood is expressed by the words truth, genuineness, reality, sincerity. Analyze manhood to its final element, and what we all mean by it is that a man is true, genuine, sincere, real. How do you find it, and where do you find it? If a man is a tradesman, and is a manly man, there is no sand in his sugar, no chicory in his coffee, no iron filings in his tea, no water in his molasses, nor does he make his marmalade of turnips and treacle. If the butcher is a manly man, he sends to your house the piece of meat you bought, and not the inferior article you did not buy. The manly man keeps his contract, make or lose—yea, he swears to his own hurt and changes not. If he builds you a house it will not be of materials as cheap as can possibly hold together, so that after it has settled you can neither fasten a window nor lock a door! The houses he builds are built to *last*. The manly man does not put all the big strawberries on the top, and all the shrunken ones at the bottom of the basket. If he sells apples, the barrel is not topped off with large and choice fruit, while in the center of the barrel they are only fit for the cider-press. The manly man, if he is an exporter of wheat to foreign ports, does not mix enough " No. 3 Red " with " No. 2 Red " to keep it within the latter grade, and at the same time have the advantage of the higher price. The manly man, even if he be a preacher in an interior town, will not sell to an ungodly buyer from New York city a lot of apples with a large pumpkin in the center of each barrel to fill up. The manly man does not sell oleomargarine for butter, neither does he manufacture his " best California honey " from glucose. The manly man is one who, if he be a large coal operator, will not sell a barge of slate for the best Lehigh coal; nor will he show you one ticket and dexterously substitute another for it on the day of election. If the manly man is a lawyer, he will not encourage litigation that he may have a fee ; if he is a broker on the Stock Exchange, he will not invent or spread false reports in order that he may further his own speculations ; if he is a physician, he will not assume an attitude of owl-like gravity when there is nothing the matter with the child; if he is a preacher, he will not have two creeds, one to work with before the people and one to think by in his study; if a manly man is in society, he will not be a retailer of cowardly slander. The manly man, wherever he is found, is a true man, a genuine man, a real man, a man who, without asking time to hide any thing away, can open his heart's most secret chamber to the angels of God any hour in the twenty-four!

This is the kind of men we need now. Acuteness of moral perception, genuineness of moral feeling, straightness of moral purpose, soundness of moral fiber through and through—in these and like elements does manhood inhere. The true man is a man, and the false man is no man; he is a two-legged snake that by some strange freak of evolution finds himself in an erect posture. Wherever there is insincerity, wherever there is equivocation, wherever there is evasion, wherever there is pretense, wherever there is gross sensuality, wherever there is falseness at the core of being—*there* is no manhood; the serpent is there, the panther is there, the tiger is there, the leopard is there—the man is still an animal, and not a man. Manhood includes other gracious, winsome, and attractive qualities, but these constitute its life and soul. Wherever there is ideal manhood there will be loyalty, magnanimity, generosity, delicacy, courtesy. Our great President and greater man, Abraham Lincoln, all unconscious of what he did, defined Christian manliness in those great and ever-memorable words: "With malice toward none, and with charity for all, let us strive to do the right, as God shall give us to see the right."

This Christian manliness we describe as sovereign, as ruling over all the elements of human life, as being the inspiration at last of all its progress, and the only ground of hope for the ages to come. It is so because the moral Ruler of men intended it to be. The reason and ground of its unique and imperial place is to be ascertained in its origin; it is the will of God that it should be so. It is the child of a King. Now this manliness is not a modern upstart usurper; it did not spring up in a night like a mushroom; it was not born yesterday. Its rule is ancient, legitimate, rightful; it is a divinely appointed sovereign. It is not a question of family; you need not look into any genealogical tables. You will waste your time there. The extraction of our heroes and heroines may not be traced in any peerage book. The men and women, far away from the world's eye, who hold themselves true to the simple duty known to them, through toilsome, suffering, unrequited years, at the cost of all those things which are grateful to the flesh, who shall describe them? They are fitly described in the superb language of Macaulay, when in the full glow of youthful eloquence he writes of the Puritans of the time of the first Charles: " If they are unacquainted with the works of philosophers and poets, they are deeply read in the oracles of God. If their names are not found in the registers of heralds, they are recorded in the Book of Life. If their steps are not accompanied by a splendid train of menials, legions of ministering angels have charge over them. Their palaces are houses not made with hands, their diadems crowns of glory that shall never fade away. On the rich and the eloquent, on nobles and priests, they look down with contempt, for they esteem themselves rich in a more precious treasure and eloquent in a more sublime language—nobles by the right of an earlier creation, and priests by the imposition of a mightier hand." The hero of our manliness is one who, in any great crisis of history, is equal to the hour that time has struck in its solemn on-goings. David is King of Israel, not because he is the son of Jesse, but because he can command the people and unify the nation in a time of separation, weakness, and distress. This manhood does not posture itself into greatness; it does not smirk itself into favor; it does not wear blazing jewels to show its rank; it does not strike theatrical attitudes before the people; it does not have an oiled curl hanging down the forehead as a proof of eminent statesmanship. This kind of manhood rules by other than artificial and meretricious badges, distinctions, and signs. It has a native, intrinsic, and inviolable majesty, and it rules because it has the ethical power to command obedience. I am glad that there are such gewgaws and baubles in the world as ivory thrones and purple robes and golden scepters. There are some people whom you would never suspect of being kings and queens if they were not seated on ivory thrones, if purple robes were not thrown around them, if golden scepters were not in their hands. Genuine manhood, if it condescends at all to sit on thrones, wear purple robes, or wield scepters, does so because of its power to dignify these things, and the real manhood requires no ermine to make a judge, no gown or surplice to make a minister of Christ—it requires nothing but the sublime instinct of faith in the eternal God, and in his righteous purpose at last to bring forth to the view of all men the clear equities of the eternities ! The sovereignty of this manhood is universal. It reigns every-where—in the church and on the street, in the academy and the prison-house, in the Senate and the market, in the Orient and in the Occident; it is superior to climate, to the aspects of nature, to rank, to genius, to talent, to wealth, to poverty, to fame, to obscurity, to suffering, to toil, to temptation, and triumphs at last over death. Wherever there is a soul that meekly bows itself in lowly reverence before the great fact that the moral law is the supreme law, *there* is a soul on its way to eternal power and growth.

This is a strange prisoner here before Pilate! They are calling him a king from the outside, and the perplexed, bewildered, time-serving Pilate says to him : " Art thou then a king ?" and his answer is : " To this end was I born, and for this cause came I into the world, that I should bear witness unto the truth." Why is he there ? He is there because he bore witness to the truth, and for no other reason. He did indeed speak the truth, and he spoke the whole truth, and he spoke nothing but the truth. If he had not been born for this one purpose, if he had not come into the world for this single end, and if he had not been faithful to his trust, he might not have stood there at all. If he had cheapened the truth, if he had lowered its imperative demands, if he had clipped off the sharp edges of the truth here and there, if he had delivered such truth only as would have been grateful to the Pharisees or to the people or to the Herodians, he would not have been there. The people might have saved him, but at times he spoke such distasteful truth to them that they turned away from him; he spoke such truth to the Pharisees that they would not have him for their leader; as he justified John the Baptist, Herod would have no pleasure in him; he refused to beg for his life at the hands of Pilate, and so he cared nothing about him. He came into the world and actually *was* the truth; that is the simple explanation, humanly speaking, of his marvelous life. He spoke the entire truth, kindly, lovingly, courageously, directly; to the rich, to the poor, to the virtuous, to the unvirtuous, to the learned, to the unversed, to those in power and to their subjects, and to all of them it was ever the same message, that is, the simple, brave truth, and nothing else. *That* is why he is a prisoner here before Pilate, and that is why all men who have really followed him have suffered, because they spoke the truth, the needed truth, the simple truth, the wholesome truth. Nevertheless *he* is, after all, the real King. Pilate! he has gone down to utter infamy. The Prisoner! he is the King of more brave, truehearted, loyal souls at this hour than any Roman emperor ever numbered subjects. As Napoleon said at St. Helena, "There are more men at this hour who would die for Jesus Christ than ever would have died for Julius Cæsar, Charlemagne, or myself."

"Every one who is of the truth heareth my voice." Would you hear that voice? Cast out every thing that corrupts, that weakens, that stains and defiles you, and you *will* hear it. Be *true*, and you will hear it. Be *true;* be true in politics, be true in the store, be true in the bank, be true in the family, be true whatever, be true wherever, you are, and you will hear His voice. " Every one that is of the truth heareth my voice." Solemn words, these! Look on this truth on its reverse side : " He that heareth not my voice, it is because the truth is not in him." If the shadow of a conscious lie lies across your soul; if you are meditating flight from duty; if you are planning one single escape from rightdoing; if along the future of your life you are leaving here and there an open door for falseness and baseness; if you would meanly undermine a competitor; if you would drive a man to the wall in the hour of weakness; if you are planning any low trick of cunning—you will not hear his voice, no, not in this world, nor yet in the world to come. But if the purpose be in your heart humbly to do right; always to do it; lovingly to do it; to be just and fear not, to be generous, to be courageous, to dare at all times to be simply true, above all other voices you will hear his voice in the holy places of your soul. Thus hearing him, and daily perfecting your obedience to him, you will go from light to light, from truth to truth, from strength to strength, from grace to grace, from virtue to virtue, from glory to glory, until, dropping the cerements of the flesh, with speed swifter than light you will rise to stand before him, and your life shall be eternally united to his life.

CHRISTIAN MANLINESS—AS TESTED BY POVERTY.

Now when Jesus saw great multitudes about him, he gave commandment to depart unto the other side. And a certain scribe came, and said unto him, Master, I will follow thee whithersoever thou goest. And Jesus saith unto him, The foxes have holes, and the birds of the air have nests; but the Son of man hath not where to lay his head.—Matt. viii, 18-20.

THIS incident occurred in the earlier and more popular portion of the Galilean ministry of Jesus. He had indeed been rudely and savagely rejected, and his life attempted by his fellow-townsmen at Nazareth, but in Capernaum, which from henceforth became his head-quarters, he had produced an immediate, deep, and, on the whole, a favorable, impression. In fact, he so profoundly moved the people by his words and by his miracles that they were frequently on the verge of a great uprising, threatening to make him a temporal king. This infectious spirit of enthusiasm in the ever-swelling crowd was at times so remarkable that it did not afford our Lord pause even for rest, solitude, and prayer. In one of these instances, when the eager, mercurial, and excited crowd thronged about him, and he sorely needed the refreshment of soul that could only come from solitude and communion with his Father, and he was about to cross the sea with his disciples in a boat, there came to him a certain scribe, a man learned in the Jewish law, who seems to have been suddenly taken with a fire of exuberant devotion, and he said unto him, "Master, I will follow thee whithersoever thou goest." It may have been that this was a transport of generous and uncalculating devotion, it may have been a sudden impulse, a mere flame-jet of fierce and untried zeal; whatever it was, it was necessary for him to know what was the real nature and demands of the service to which the Master would lead him, and Jesus therefore declared to him his utter poverty: "The foxes have holes, and the birds of the air have nests; but the Son of man hath not where to lay his head." Do you want to follow such a man? Are you prepared for such a service? Are you equal to such a discipleship?

As men estimate power and influence, these words of Jesus must have seemed very foolish and shortsighted indeed. "Why," they must have said among themselves, "here is this scribe, versed in the law, having potential connections—he may be able to give a favorable introduction to this new teacher in influential quarters; perhaps he may be able to present this new doctrine among the great and wise men who live in the city of Jerusalem, and such hard and unpalatable words ought not to be spoken to him, standing as he does on the very threshold of the new kingdom, and eager to enter it." But, with Jesus, here as elsewhere, now as always, there was no compromise, no lowering of the standard, no truce with the world spirit, no equivocation, no evasion, no hiding or obscuring of the truth. The man needed to understand what was involved in his choice, and so Jesus said to him: " I am poor; my life, and the life of those who company with me, is to be a life of stern poverty, yea, of wandering and homeless poverty; I am not as well off as the beasts of the field and the fowls of the air: the fox has a hole in which he may seek security and refuge and rest, which is his home; the birds of the air have their snug dwelling-places, their warm nests; but as for me, there is no place that I dare call my own; *the Son of man hath not where to lay his head."*

We see here the perfect Man in poverty, the perfect Man in *actual* poverty, rising superior to the malign elements, the limitations and stings of that state; and this raises for us the fruitful theme of Christian manliness in poverty. Let us consider some of the difficulties, the besetments, the hinderances, the tests interposed by poverty in the development of an ideal manhood. There is danger to a lofty Christian manliness in the false, and I fear the growing, idea (growing certainly in some portions of American society) that poverty is a necessary shame and an inherent disgrace, a token and a badge of social dishonor. There *is* indeed dishonorable poverty, disgraceful poverty, poverty of which a true man may be justly ashamed—a poverty that is the fruit of idleness, a poverty that is the result of vice, a poverty that is the result of laziness; there is no intrinsic honor, no inherent virtue, in a poverty which is the result either of laziness, or of vice, or of shiftlessness. But where poverty is not the retributive issue of dissipation, or idleness, or crime; where, by no act of folly or wastefulness, by no course of carelessness, no sin or crime of our own, poverty comes to us by causes over which we have absolutely no control—as where we are born to it—then there is nothing in poverty intrinsically disgraceful or shameful. So far from this, there is a poverty that comes to men sometimes that is the immediate occasion or reason for that splendid forth-putting of irresistible energy which first brings to real men a regal sense of themselves. When, however, a youth begins to look upon poverty as a badge of shame, as a token of social disgrace, he at once opens every gate of his soul to the entrance of the enemy, to all manner of temptations—the temptation to evasion, to pretense, to seeming, to concealment, to equivocation, to falsehood—and the perils of his situation will soon appear. In his endeavor to associate with those whose means are far beyond his own, and where he must necessarily—if he means to dress as they do, if he means to have such amusements as they have, if he means to mingle in such pleasures as they do—he must necessarily be encouraging dishonest thoughts and secretly meditating crooked courses; for neither his income, nor his wardrobe, nor his business, nor his prospects, nor any thing in his present circumstances will justify him in attempting to live beyond his means. Woe to the young men who, regarding poverty as a shame and a disgrace, are striving to wear such clothes, to mingle with such people, to go into that kind of society where it will soon become necessary for them to lie and steal in order to keep up appearances.

He who would preserve his manhood in poverty must have a serene faith and an invincible courage. Poverty, especially to certain men, to men with a certain order or balance of faculty, moral and intellectual, suggests doubts of the absolute equity of God's moral rule over the world and men. It may be in earlier years, it may be at a time when poverty pinches closely and sharply; but, however brought about, there can be no doubt that some men endowed with a high degree of thinking power, born in such poverty, do come sooner or later to the place where they will at least wonder why they were born so empty and poor, and so many weak, useless, incapable, undeserving people were born rich. And when this wonder grows into doubt, and this doubt is allowed to remain with us, when we harbor it, when we feed it, when we nurse it, when we strengthen it, when we allow it to smother energy and truth, when we begin to adopt practically, without knowing the meaning of the word, the philosophy of pessimism—that every thing is bad, and going to the bad—then poverty is acting like moral poison. My young friends, I would be entirely frank with you. There are a great many things here we do not understand. I have sent many puzzling questions, as well as many dear friends, into the other life. I fear not to leave to him who is our Father any question that is too hard for me. Life, with work and trust, is ever so much better than slow death from the poison of a swarm of stinging interrogation points. We must never allow ourselves to doubt that at the center of the universe is absolute equity. Come whatever doubts may, come whatever hardships may, no matter how much we are puzzled by things on which, with our feeble thought-power, we can throw no revealing light—we must always believe that at the center of the universe there is eternal rectitude. We must believe that, or we shall die of heart-break. Whatever happens to us, however dark the day, however leaden the sky, however heavy the burden, however long and lonely the night, however bitter the disciplines through which we must pass, we must believe that the Judge of all the earth will at last, somehow, somewhere, do right to all his children.

If we mean to carry our manhood uncorrupted through the state of poverty, we will need also to be brave men; not cowardly men, not men who will shrink, not men who will flee the battle. We need to have the rare quality called moral courage, and, above all, we must not rail at the world. Do not sit down in the ashes and wail and mourn and lament. What business have we, sons of God in disguise, awaiting the hour of our disclosure, to sit down by the " poisoned springs of life, waiting for the morrow that shall free us from the strife?"

I know that the world looks dark to some of you,

but I know also that the men who bravely front it, and fear not to look it full in the face, and fight it, will find that it is not such a bad world after all. Do not imitate the man who, because of repeated disappointments, fell into the habit of railing at the world, and finally declared that, if he had been a hatter, he was sure men would have been born without heads. We all need to buy a new dictionary, and, if possible, I hope every one of you will get a copy of the same edition General Grant is said to have had when he was a boy; the one in which, as he told his father once, he could not find the word " can't." I am informed that this was the copy he took with him through the war, and I am half inclined to believe it. The man who says, " I can't," confesses and brands himself a coward. With his own hand he burns the brand deep in his own flesh. Don't!

There is a flood of temptations assailing Christian manliness coming in from another quarter, especially when bright young men suddenly find themselves in poverty, without friends, and with no immediate prospect of pecuniary independence. These may be described by the general statement that they are slyly and plausibly solicited to rely upon smartness, upon cunning tricks, upon sharp dealings, upon brilliant strokes, rather than upon quiet, steady, solid, faithful, honest, hard work. This class of temptations is peculiarly insinuating to those who have a quick, facile, and showy understanding, and have never learned to work. God pity the young man with an alert brain who does not know how to do something with his hands! Is it unfashionable? Then let me be forever out of style. I am a follower in this matter of the old Jewish rabbis who declared, " He who raises his son without a trade raises him to be a thief." In the complex conditions of modern life, especially in great cities, the young man who reaches his majority not having learned to work, that is, not having learned to do something which the world really needs, and to do that something well—I do not mean now merely a mechanical craft, although it would be a great blessing if more of our young men were mechanics—I mean something the world must have done by somebody. I say that the young man who has reached his majority and cannot do something in this sense is in a weak, helpless, and most pitiable condition. I declare that he who has not yet learned the value of industry, he who is studying to be an adventurer, a moral gambler, a gamester, a sharp speculator—the young man who is planning and scheming to live on his wits without work—is on his way to the penitentiary. In nine cases out of ten, if the laws are enforced, that is precisely where he will land. Remember that for every honest fortune suddenly made, a hundred fortunes are slowly made; remember that in times of commercial crash the sudden fortunes almost always go first, and the slowly built fortunes weather the storm; remember that for every man who makes a great and sudden success there is sure to be a paragraph in the newspapers, while the same newspapers make little account of quiet, patient worth and honest industry; remember that the lasting reputations in every department of professional activity are the slowly built, solid reputations; remember that when God means to bless men by riches he does it as he blesses the earth by rain. The gentle rain, continued through days, penetrates the soil and soaks the roots; the sudden, dashing rain only moistens the surface of the ground. Beware of the wealth that comes like a dashing storm! It will never reach the roots of your being.

Christian manliness is menaced also by the temptation to believe that happiness, growth, strength, are to be sought and found rather in what men have than in what men are. There is no mistake among young men more wide-spread, none more fatal, none more false, than the belief that what men have constitutes happiness, growth, strength; and there is nothing more demoralizing. There are a great many young men who are saying to themselves, "If I lived in that house over there, if I just had that man's income, I would be happy." There are a great many foolish young men who think that Mr. Vanderbilt sleeps ten hours out of the twenty-four, while, if the truth were known, there are few men in America who sleep fewer hours, sleep less lightly and less refreshingly. The idea that wealth is an unmixed blessing is a mistake. Wealth once acquired must be kept, and how difficult that is let them describe who have tried!

When a man gets a fortune, at once all sorts of people want to know him; he has more friends than he ever dreamed of before; he has more subscription papers thrust under his eyes than ever before, and he must indeed be glib of tongue and quick of hand and fleet of foot to escape the one half of them; that is the time when all of his relatives, near and remote, and all his wife's relatives, near and remote, are anxious to establish close family relations; that is the time when a man's life is fairly badgered and worried out of him by people who have no sort of claim upon him. This idea that heaven consists in possessing wealth! My friends, my friends, we carry hell or heaven about with us in our own breasts, and we will never find it any place else; it is not outside of us, and it never will be. I speak with reverence, but God himself could not put a good man in hell; there is no hell for the good man—you cannot conceive of one; he would make what you call hell a heaven. I repeat it: There is no hell for the good man.

One day when our Lord was teaching, and a great crowd of people were gathered about him, suddenly his discourse was interrupted by a man who came out of the crowd and said, "Master, speak to my brother, that he divide the inheritance with me." He was a man who supposed that if he could once secure an equitable division of his father's estate all his troubles would at once disappear, all his wrongs would be righted, and henceforth the world would be just about what it ought to be.

So he came to Jesus, but Jesus refused to have any thing to do with him. He never interfered in any personal, political, or domestic difficulties. I do not now recall a single instance of his having done so. He looked at him and said, "Man, who made me a judge or divider over you?" Then he turned from the man to the great crowd, and said, "Take heed and beware of covetousness" (that is, beware of greed for money), "for a man's life" (his true life, his real life) "consisteth not in the abundance of the things which he possesseth." Then he spoke the parable of the rich man whose grounds brought forth plentifully, and he tore down his old, rickety barns, and built new barns, which he filled to overflowing, and then, seating himself on a large easy chair, he stroked himself with great satisfaction, and said to himself, "Soul, eat, drink, and be merry; thou hast much goods laid up for many years." He had scarcely finished his soliloquy when quick through the silent night came the awful voice of God: "Thou fool, this night thy soul shall be required of thee; then whose shall those things be which thou hast provided? So is every one that is not rich toward God."

Are these obstacles surmountable? Are these difficulties removable? Are these temptations conquerable? Do you know of any man or men who have stood in poverty, beset by temptations like these, and kept their manhood uncorrupted? About seventy-five years ago, far away in the granite hills of New Hampshire, a little tow-headed boy had a hard time of it wading through the snow-drifts two and three feet deep to the rude school-house. His parents lived in a rough, unpainted, one-story frame house, and what little he really learned he acquired from his wise and intelligent mother, a woman who filled his memory and fired his imagination with the thrilling stories of the Scotch-Irish settlement in the north of Ireland. One Monday morning at sunrise a strange experience came into this boy's life, for the sheriff and the chief creditor of his father came, and as they knocked at the front door his father disappeared at the rear door, and was invisible the remainder of the day; then the creditor and the sheriff began to seize on the goods in the presence of the family, until finally a friend and neighbor came and took them away in a wagon from the scene of their sorrow and shame. Then they tried it in Vermont, and they had a hard time of it there, and at fifteen years of age he had to go to Poultney to learn the printing trade, where he indentured himself for five years. His father could not make things go in Vermont, and so he concluded to go out into the western part of New York, and hew himself a home out of the virgin forest. The boy walked twelve miles out from Poultney to say good-bye; and although they had had hard times together he would have been quite willing to have gone with them (if his mother had asked him) but for one reason—that is, he would not break faith with his employer. So he said good-bye to them, and walked back to Poultney. He said it was the slowest and saddest walk of his life, and we may well believe him. He stayed there until he had learned his trade, and then he went west and helped his father chop the trees, occasionally working at his trade. Finally, when he had fifty dollars, he thought it was time to go to New York, so he divided the fifty dollars, giving his father twenty-five and keeping twenty-five himself. He walked to Albany, and came down from there on the boat. After landing, he walked up to the corner of Wall and Broad Streets, and entered a boarding-house, where they told him the price of board was six dollars a week. He said, "I can't afford to pay that" (there are not a great many young men nowadays who are not able to pay any price for board), so he walked about until he found a boarding-house on West Street where he could live for two dollars and a half a week. It was not an inviting place; they sold liquor below, but he was a teetotaler, and they gave him fair bread and butter, and he stayed there. He started in business several times, and failed several times, but always paid his debts. He made several publishing ventures, and finally on a day of "most unseasonable chill and sleet and snow," in the year 1841, some newsboys cried out, "*New York Tribune*, one cent a copy!" Then began the great work of his life, and for more than thirty years he formed and directed public opinion. He did not find out what public opinion was and then record it, but he created public opinion; he molded it, gave it impulse and direction, and at last met the fate of many of the world's great men, being hounded and hunted to death chiefly by men whose power and publicity he had made possible. He died an uncrowned king, but the tears of a nation were his monument. And this is the triumph of manhood over poverty in the life of Horace Greeley in America in the nineteenth century.

It is not true in the North only. About sixty-five years ago, in the South, there was an orphan in Georgia who was poor, but bright, acquisitive, full of mental eagerness, and the Georgia Educational Society heard about him, and sent him to school, and he went through college. He was graduated, and the most remarkable thing about his early career was that as soon as he earned the money he paid back to the Georgia Educational Society what they had loaned him. That is more than some young preachers have done—paid back to the eleemosynary and other societies the funds loaned them to procure collegiate and seminary training. He began to practice law, and he did what, in that section of the country, meant a good deal more than it ever did in this section of the country—he swept his own office, he built his own fires, he blacked his own boots, and he managed to live on six dollars a month. When his first important case came on he went to the county-seat to try it, and, finding that he did not have sufficient means to go to the hotel where the other lawyers were stopping, he arranged his toilet in the woods outside of the town, his horse tied to a tree. His toilet made, he went in and won the suit. He saved up money until he bought back the homestead which his father had lost. He did good as opportunity afforded, taking more than fifty young men from the common school and helping them through college, paying the entire expenses of twenty young men of unusual promise. I never saw him but once—a poor, feeble, broken-down, attenuated old man, with the stigma upon him of having been a conspicuous leader of an unsuccessful rebellion, rolled about in the House of Representatives in his invalid chair; but when, in that thin, shrill, piping voice, he said, " Mr. Speaker, Mr. Speaker," James A. Garfield and other Republican leaders ran down the aisle to hear what Alexander H. Stephens had to say. Essential manliness knows no North, no South, no circumstances, no conditions. Wherever it finds itself in the world, it fights its battles and wins its victories.

Nor these alone, for there are many in humble life who have fought life's battle and won; whose names are not recorded in human history, albeit they are recorded in that Book where nothing good or great or noble is ever forgotten. There once was a boy in a printing-office, an apprentice, and the boys in the shop said he was penurious, mean, niggardly, because he would not take part in their " treats." If they wanted beer, to use the phraseology of that shop, he would not " chip in ;" if they wanted ice-cream, he would not contribute any thing to the expense. They thought it was mean and contemptible, and they followed him one day and saw him go into a cheap bakery and buy some bread, and they followed him up-stairs where there was an old, feeble mother and a blind sister, and then they knew that the stuff was in him out of which you make heroes. Hugh Miller said of the master-mason to whom he was apprenticed that "he never laid a stone without putting his conscience into it." That man was a hero! Poor, are you? And do you know how many great men have been poor? Paul, the apostle to the Gentiles, was poor and a tent-maker; Hildebrand, the great ecclesiastical statesman, afterward Gregory VII., the greatest of the popes, was poor; Martin Luther was the son of a North Saxon miner, and poor. Have you heard of Jeremy Taylor, whose pen dropped gold, and of Sir Richard Arkwright, the inventor of the spinning-jenny, and of Turner, the great landscape-painter? They all graduated from the barber-shop. Poor, are you? Shakespeare's father was a grazier, and Cardinal Wolsey's was a butcher; Ben Jonson worked with a trowel in his hand and a book in his pocket. Poor, are you? Faraday was apprenticed to a bookbinder until he was twenty-two years of age; Sir William Herschel began life as a hautboy-player in a regimental band; Claude Lorraine, the great French landscape-painter, was first an apprentice to a pastry cook; John Bunyan was a tinker; Copernicus was the son of a Polish baker; Richard Cobden was a London warehouse boy, whose masters told him not to waste too much time in reading. Poor, are you? Do you know that Ben

Franklin was the son of a Boston tallow-chandler? And Patrick Henry, by whose fiery and resistless eloquence Virginia was swept into the tide of the Revolution, was poor; and William Henry Harrison was poor; and Henry Wilson was poor; and Abraham Lincoln was poor; and James A. Garfield was poor. Empty this church of the men who were poor first, and it could not sustain itself as a second-rate mission-chapel! Empty New York of the men who were first poor, and you would paralyze its greatest enterprises! Poor, are you? Poverty means to the man who has the genuine material in him out of which men are made, the opportunity to force victory from apparent defeat, and despite obscurity and ill-health and lack of friends, and the great world's stony indifference, to fight his way to the front.

"The foxes have holes, and the birds of the air have nests, but the Son of man hath not where to lay his head." The poverty of Jesus was not feigned; it was real, actual. I do not understand how so many people can believe in the New Testament and interpret it in the way they do. If I thought these words were feigned, that they were words of simulation, it would take the very heart out of them for me. If these words are to be taken in an accommodated sense, as many people seem to believe; if Jesus was not really poor, and simply pretended that he was, why, then, away with him! If the tears he wept were dramatic tears, he is no helper to me when mine flow like rain. His poverty was real as his sorrow was real, it was real as his loneliness was real, it was real as his betrayal by friends was real, it was as real as any act or experience of that marvelous divine life in the flesh! It was not a seeming, fictitious, theatrical poverty, it was a real poverty, the genuine poverty of One who deliberately chose it, of One who, "being rich, for our sakes became poor." And when he chose poverty it was an actual, straitening, pinching poverty; and therefore I say that he is in full and gracious sympathy with all who are in poverty and are struggling to be manly. "Forasmuch as his brethren partook of flesh and blood, he also himself likewise took part of the same." He was tempted (tested) in all points, just as we are being tested daily. Therefore I present him to you as your Captain, your Leader, your Brother, your Friend, in every effort to maintain manhood in poverty, loneliness, discouragement, and depression. Do not be a whiner. Do not be a murmurer. Do not be an adventurer. Do not be a sneak. Do not nominate and elect yourself as a martyr. Do not rail at the world. Up and at it! Do your best! You can fight, and you can, if need be, die trying to be dutiful, loving, true. And Jesus will help you to win the fight. Obey him, follow him, enlist under his banner. He has never led a soldier anywhere to permanent loss and defeat. Who would fear to trust himself to a Pilot who in every sort of craft, in every stress of weather, had safely sailed in every sea? He comes from the highest Heaven, our glorious Captain, first being made in all things like unto his brethren, and lo! he marches out into the "open field of the great world, carrying the victorious standard which shall never go back." Believe him, obey him, trust him, and he will conduct you to eternal triumph and honor and power.

CHRISTIAN MANLINESS—AS PUT TO THE PROOF IN PUBLIC LIFE.

When Jesus therefore perceived that they would come and take him by force, to make him a king, he departed again into a mountain himself alone.—John vi, 15.

I AM to speak to you to-night of Manhood in Public Life. In this country, with our popular methods of political action, with the very air itself instinct with the spirit of democracy, under our elastic forms of social and political action, every citizen, at some time or other in the course of his life, must expect to be called to the performance of some public duties. In fact, every time we cast a ballot we have entered public life. The casting of a ballot, under a political system such as ours, is not a private act; it is an act that has a certain and more or less intimate relation to the common weal, and our ballot stands for our opinion as to the right policies or the right men required for the duties of the time. Every man who is worthily a holder and exerciser of the right of suffrage is by so much a public man, being bound to think not only of his personal welfare and protection, but of the security and happiness of all who are joined with him in this political society. We have in this country, happily, no hereditary ruling class, no established Church, no privileged office-holding class, and I wish I could say no chartered monopolies, but, alas! I cannot; and such are the conditions of public life, such is the nature of our political institutions, that their gifts, their honors, their emoluments, their powers are open to all who are pleased to strive for them. It is the duty, therefore, of every citizen of a representative republic to prepare himself, as far as in him lies, to respond to such calls as may be made on him by his fellow-citizens, so that he may serve the State with capacity, fidelity, and honor. It is the more necessary to say these things because one of the dangers of the day is the lurking belief that between high character, and especially high character in the religious sense, and political or public life there is necessary incompatibility. So far as this opinion still obtains it is a dangerous opinion. I am quite sure that it largely obtained in the community in which I grew up, and especially among the religious portion of the community. To such an extent did it prevail that, while it was thought that a man might be a lawyer and get to heaven, it was almost universally believed that a man could not be a politician and get to heaven. It was thought necessary, in order to attain any eminence in religious character, that one should separate himself from the profession of the law, and certainly from any kind of active participation in public affairs. Such teaching has not been confined to provincial villages. The eminent Dr. Dewey, delivering some profound lectures before the Lowell Institute, made a digression to call upon some eminent member of the legal profession to rescue his profession from the unjust reproaches that had fallen upon it as being unfriendly to the development of high character.

All this is a part of the luggage that Protestantism brought with it when it moved out from Rome; for we did not escape whole—we brought out with us a good many things that belonged to the Egyptians. We brought with us—and we have not yet fully escaped its thralldom—the mediæval ecclesiastical idea that life is to be divided into two parts, one called secular and the other religious; a distinction nowhere recognized in the New Testament, and entirely foreign to the whole spirit of the life and teachings of Jesus Christ. The attempt to make one day religious and another secular, to make one building sacred and another secular, to make one act holy and another secular, is a part and parcel of that system of mediævalism from which we have not wholly escaped. There can be no secular days to a truly religious man, for the consecration of any day depends upon the consecration of the man, and wherever there is present the ruling divine Spirit, all days are religious, all buildings are consecrated, all acts are noble. There must, therefore, come to men more and more this great truth of life, that, so far from there being any incompatibility between high character and political action, Christ meant to develop and perfect the type of character to which he calls us, IN the world, and not out of the world.

If additional justification be needed for the topic of the evening, it may be found in the undeniable and discouraging fact that on the part of many educated, refined, and virtuous persons in the community there is a startling indifference to, sometimes an almost criminal neglect of, their civic duties. Those of you who have at any recent period attended any political conventions must have been surprised, first at the men who were there, and next at the men who were not there. If ever you have made a study of how these cities are governed, and most other American cities, if ever you have made a study of those who practically control the politics of this country in the large centers of population, you are aware of the fact of which the men who are trying to purify the politics of our cities have long been painfully aware; namely, that while on the one hand the ignorant, the venal, the corrupt, the debased are swift to avail themselves of all political privileges, the classes who are criminal in the neglect of their political duties are generally those most competent, intellectually and morally, to perform the same. It can no longer be doubted that in the majority of the great cities of America the saloon, its influence and agents, stands for a mightier power in municipal affairs than the churches and the school-houses. The statistics that have been gathered, the observations made by men free from narrowness, bigotry, and prejudice, show conclusively that the saloon, and that for which it stands, is exercising more power in our large cities than all the churches and school-houses combined. What does this mean? It means that in these cities, at least, we are hastening to a government of the worst; it means, unless the evil be speedily corrected, the death of such political institutions as we now have, for such institutions cannot long survive if the government is practically in the hands of the worst element in the community.

I will not longer delay, in passing, to unfold or discuss the peculiar perils of public life in such a democratic community as ours; they are sufficiently indicated by such words as sycophancy, cowardice, insincerity, demagogy, trickery, deceitful handling of the truth, venality, envy, selfishness, flattery, and, above all, the worship of the new and popular god called "Success."

It is possible for men to enter and remain in public life, and have sterling manliness. One night, in the city of London, when John Stuart Mill was addressing an audience of working-men, desiring their votes to return him to Parliament, a man arose and interrupted him, holding a book in his hand, and asked Mr. Mill if he had not at such a time published a certain book in which he used the following language, in substance; namely, That one marked characteristic of the workmen of that part of the city of London was lying. "Now, Mr. Mill," said the inquirer, "did you write this?" And John Stuart Mill, straightening himself up to his full height, looking full in the face the men whose votes were to decide the question, calmly and quietly answered, "I did." How many men in America would first bring such a charge against the electors, and then, when the time came to answer for it, on the very eve of election, nobly confess that they had made the charge, and offer no word of cowardly apology for their statement? During the long and famous controversy in the State of Massachusetts that finally sent Charles Sumner to the United States Senate, he was again and again solicited by over-anxious friends to make his appearance at the capitol, and at least to shake hands with some of the electors, but he quietly and persistently refused to go near the place or to have any dealings, directly or indirectly, with the men who were to determine the question. He never stooped to solicit votes to seat him in the United States Senate. Think of it! Men used to be elected to the United States Senate on account of their superior intelligence and pure character without any personal solicitation of votes! Yes, it is true, incredulous as it may sound to some of you. Alas! that class of senators is nearly gone! And when this man reached the United States Senate they had great difficulty to classify him, because he refused to commit himself to any party, to any convention, to any junta, and when it was proposed by some one in the Senate to give him proper recognition on the committees, Mr. Jefferson Davis, a senator from Mississippi, rose and objected on the ground that the senator from Massachusetts was outside of all healthy political organizations.

In some respects the greatest name in English politics and English literature in the last century was Edmund Burke. He carried into politics two forces not always found there—genius and conscience. He loved the right; he had a simple faith in it; he served it; he would not do it violence. When the city of Bristol, in 1774, made him their representative in Parliament the gentleman who was chosen before him, with hasty and indecent subservience, assured the Bristol merchants that he would be delighted always to carry out their mandates. Burke, following him, took occasion to tell the Bristol electors that he would carry out their mandates only so far as they were approved by his conscience and judgment. It happened that in 1778 a measure came up in Parliament to relax slightly the hitherto atrocious fiscal policy of England toward Ireland. All the great commercial communities were interested in it, and the Bristol merchants came to Burke with theis urgent pleas, beseeching him to vote against the bill; but he was superior to British greed, and plainly told them that he saw no reason why the grasping policy of England toward Ireland should any longer be pursued. In the same year it was proposed to repeal some of the iniquitous acts against the Roman Catholics, whereupon the religious zealots were aroused, and they sent a deputation to Burke to oppose any such liberal measure; but as he was for humanity in dealing with Ireland so he was for toleration to the Catholics, and bravely voted to repeal the iniquitous laws. And then they discovered that he had been bred at St. Mary's, that he was a papist in disguise, and that in all human probability he was a Jesuit! Is it any wonder that Edmund Burke, with his clear apprehension of the right, and his fiery and glowing devotion to it, with his absolute faith in the final supremacy of ethical forces, joined to his magnificent powers, should become the master of the most superb and commanding eloquence?

In the early part of this century there was a man in England who, in some respects, was to English politics and literature what Burke had been in the last century. Both Macaulay and Burke were men of genius; they both loved literature and the " still air of delightful studies;" they both had the faith of the right, and both obeyed it. When Macaulay was thirty-two years of age, standing as a parliamentary candidate for Leeds, the electors of that city demanded of him certain pledges. In reply he wrote them the famous letter, which concludes as follows: " It is not necessary to my happiness that I should sit in Parliament, but it is necessary to my happiness that I should possess, in Parliament or out of Parliament, the consciousness of having done what is right." Three times he represented the great city of Edinburgh in the House of Commons. In the year 1847 a most disgraceful and grotesque combination of religious bigots and whisky-dealers was formed to defeat him, and the combination was successful. The religious bigots were opposed to him on the ground that he had voted to grant public money to Maynooth College, and Macaulay's defense was that so long as public money was to be granted to any religious institutions, and Roman Catholics continued to be British subjects, he would vote for such appropriations of public money to these institutions as seemed to him just and proper, whether they were under the control of Protestants or Catholics. The whisky-dealers wanted the tax on whisky reduced, and they sent a deputation to ask him to do something for them. His reply was, "Gentlemen, I can do nothing for you, and the probabilities are I will do something against you." The whisky-dealers and the religious bigots joined hands to leave at home England's greatest historian and essayist. In five years Edinburgh came to herself, got her senses back again, and sent him to Parliament without his appearing at the polls. It was this same Macaulay who denied himself to pay his father's debts; who would not go to India, at a salary of ten thousand pounds a year, unless his favorite sister, Hannah, would accompany him, and who, after a great speech in Parliament, stood cool, unmoved, and impassive, the center of an admiring and applauding crowd, but in whose eyes were the quick tears when he read the congratulatory note of his sister and niece.

And have we no such men in America? It has pleased God, in his wise and good providence, to give to this nation within the last quarter of a century a most sovereign man, a man whom Plutarch would have been delighted to have had for a hero, a man whose name is one of the ten or twelve really great names that will survive all times and civilizations, and that man is Abraham Lincoln! The whole spirit of his life is disclosed by their use of him when a young man on the western frontier. Fond of out-door athletic sports, he never could have his full share in any of the conflicts, races, or games, because his comrades were perpetually choosing him for umpire. He was too just a judge to be permitted to act as champion. It was Lincoln who wrote, and well would it be for all men if they could truthfully write the same words: "I never willingly planted a thorn in any man's bosom." It was Lincoln who so fairly stated the other side to the jury that his clients feared he would concede away their causes. It was Lincoln who said: "Certainly the negro is not our equal in color, and perhaps not in many other respects; still, in his right to put into his own mouth the bread that he earns with his own hands, I suppose that he is equal to any other man, black or white." It was Lincoln who, in a dark and stormy hour, wrote these words: "Let us hold fast the faith that right makes might, and in that faith let us dare to do our duty to the end as we understand it." Why, these are words that will be quoted thousands of years hence! These axiomatic statements, these pithy proverbs, these wonderful sayings of Abraham Lincoln are henceforth a part of the imperishable literature of mankind. They are rich with the condensed ethical wisdom of the world. It was Lincoln who steadily refused to recede from the ground taken in the Emancipation Proclamation. There are some people who pretend to have discovered that Abraham Lincoln was not orthodox, on the ground, as is alleged, that he denied the doctrine of future punishment. Lincoln once gave his consent to the doctrine of future punishment in a direct, practical way, quite strong enough to satisfy me. Certain men came to him and proposed that he should return to slavery some black soldiers, and thus conciliate the South. "There have been men base enough to propose to me to return to slavery our black warriors of Port Hudson and Olustee, and thus win the respect of the masters they fought. Should I do so, I should deserve to be damned in time and eternity. Come what will, I will keep my faith with friend and foe." Have you forgotten his patience? Have you forgotten his sympathy with the suffering? Have you forgotten his faith in the people? Have you forgotten his fatherly tenderness of disposition toward the private soldier boy? Have you forgotten his calm reliance on the vitality and invincibility of moral forces? Abraham Lincoln, the rough, unpolished diamond of the West, the man who did what neither Sumner, nor Chase, nor Seward, nor Greeley could have done: hold the heart of the whole nation to himself in the sublime conviction that he would never fail to do the right as fast and as far as he saw it, nor ever permit malice to enter his great heart! Forget him? Never! And never, so long as the sun holds his place, and the stars keep their courses, if we but remember him, and follow in his ways, need we despair of the Republic, for the soil whence he sprang is rich enough to produce other heroes, who, in times of darkness and danger, shall rescue the nation.

Will some one ask how far this is removed from the spirit of Jesus? That depends on how far you are yourself removed from the monastery! If your idea of purity, virtue, religion, is a monastic idea, you cannot, of course, see any moral connection between these truths and the spirit of Jesus; but if your idea of virtue is that it is a strong, hardy, vigorous plant, growing, not in the hot-house, but in the bright, fresh, pure air of heaven, you will not miss the connection. Jesus was a public man. From the time of his rejection by his fellow-townsmen of Nazareth, he never had a home. He had really no private or domestic life after his public work began. The foxes had holes, and the birds of the air had their nests, but he had not where to lay his head. The first temptation that assaulted Jesus as regards his public life was to be impatient. When he said to his mother at twelve years of age, " Wist ye not that I must be about my Father's business?" what does it mean but that the fore-glimpses of his public life were already dawning upon him? Nevertheless, he went down to Nazareth and remained subject unto them for eighteen years. Great is the mystery of his being! I stand before it with increasing reverence and awe! More and more do I call him my God in the flesh, but during those eighteen silent years, as he grew to manhood, and to a sense of the supreme Divinity within, he learned what every Christ-like man must learn—to be quiet and patient.

He knew what the temptation was to become the leader of a class. The poor gathered about him in great numbers; he was friendly to them, he felt their wrongs, and sympathized deeply with them, but he never became a leader of the poor. We feel that it is irreverent to compare Henry George in his championship of the poor with the attitude of Jesus to the poor. The poor of the world have never had such a friend as Jesus of Nazareth, but he never for one moment was betrayed into any thought of mere partisan leadership. He must also have been tempted to ingratiate himself with the great and powerful. We know, in fact, that it could not have been otherwise; but he silently pushed away the temptation. We know that he was tempted at one point in his life by a close friend, Peter, to adopt the spirit of the world rather than the spirit of the cross, as a means for the establishment of his kingdom. In the region of Cesarea Philippi, when Jesus announced his approaching death at Jerusalem, and began to unfold the final scene, Peter took him to one side and rebuked him, saying: "This shall not be unto thee." What was it that Jesus said in reply? "Thou savorest not the things that be of God, but the things that be of men." It was a direct temptation to rely for the success of his kingdom upon human policy and institutions, upon external agencies, upon education, literature and art, upon any thing save the cross, but he distinctly said, " No, Peter, I choose the way of the cross!" The reason why it is all so mysterious to us—the great reason why we do not penetrate the interior ranges of his truth better than we do—is because so few of us in our own lives are seeking to perfect ourselves by carrying his cross in his spirit.

He deliberately disclaimed all other sources of influence and of power, and went to his cross. He must have been strongly tempted to an extravagant and intemperate use of the peculiar supernatural powers that resided in him. You are surprised, some of you, that he raised three persons from the dead, and I am surprised, remembering who he was, that he did not raise hundreds of thousands from the dead. Surprised that he healed a leper? Are you not rather surprised that he did not heal all lepers? Have you never, in the wide sympathy of your own throbbing heart, wondered why God ever permitted a single sigh? Have you never, in the loneliness of your life, wondered why God did not cut his work short in righteousness? And when God's Son was here, with power to still the sea, to give sight to the blind, hearing to the deaf, language to the dumb, to make the lame man leap as a hart, to raise the dead—why did he not employ his power to make a perfect world? The reserved use, the sober, temperate, moral use of the peculiar powers of Divinity resident in him constitutes, to those who are without bias and prepossession, one of the most remarkable and convincing proofs that he was the eternal Son of God.

Do you believe that when the New Testament says that Jesus " hungered " he really was hungry? Do you believe that when it says that Jesus endured the ills of human life he really suffered them? Do you not believe that it was acted? Are there not here those who explain away the glorious reality of this divine life? Do you really believe that he was tempted to be a leader of the poor, to be popular with the great, and that he refused these temptations? That he was tempted to use his power showily and extravagantly, and that he rejected the temptation? The majority of people, as they read the New Testament, seem to me to resolve it into a tissue of fictions. The Christ of many people seems to be a dramatic Christ; one who simply acted a part on the stage, not one who was really in the world, and lived and suffered and was tempted as men and women now live and suffer and are tempted. Do you believe the declaration of the Epistle to the Hebrews, that he suffered, being tempted? Do you believe that the heavens now hold One who actually suffered in his temptations? Jesus was a public man, and was assaulted at the points where every public man is assaulted, and won his victory there by obedience to the will of his righteous Father.

Some young man here, contemplating a public career, has been soliloquizing with himself, and has about reached this conclusion : " Well, for my purposes, for my plan of life, for my ambitions, religion is not really a necessity; I am strong and healthy, I have a good education, I mean to write books or edit a paper or enter upon the practice of the legal profession, with a view to politics. In some way or other I mean to serve the State in a public capacity, and, so far as I am concerned, I do not need religion—it would rather be in the way. Probably there would be times and occasions when it would be seriously inconvenient to have too much religion; it might frustrate and destroy all my plans. Now, if I was weak and sickly, if I came of a consumptive family, if I was a woman, I would be religious; but as I am going to be a public man, to be a leader of my fellow-men, I will wait for my religion until the doctor tells me that there is not more than an hour and a half left, and then, of course, some kind of preparation must be made for the next world." O, vain young man! O, foolish young man! O, presumptuous young man! Religion is a necessity, even to you, and you will find it an inspiration, a constant stimulus and help. Gladstone's religion has never been inconvenient to him, Washington's religion was never inconvenient to him, Henry Wilson's religion was never inconvenient to him, Garfield's religion was never inconvenient to him, Benjamin Harrison's religion was never inconvenient to him. You can win any prize that can fairly be won, you can fill any honorable position for which you find yourself fitted, you can wield any noble form of influence which you covet, and at the same time keep your soul unspotted from the world under the leadership of Jesus Christ. We need a race of public men who are afraid to do wrong; we need a race of public men who love the right; we need a generation of public men who have faith in the final supremacy of right; we need a generation of public men who will recognize their brotherhood with Jesus Christ, and by the presence and inspiration of his Spirit walk in his footsteps, even if, as in his case, the path of duty should lead to the cross. Manliness in public life after the manner of Jesus—herein may the God of our fathers make and keep us strong!

JESUS AND THE GREAT MASTERS OF LITERATURE.

Then went the Pharisees, and took counsel how they might entangle him in his talk. And they sent out unto him their disciples with the Herodians, saying, Master, we know that thou art true, and teachest the way of God in truth, neither carest thou for any man: for thou regardest not the person of men.—Matt. xxii, 15, 16.

LITERATURE is the written record of the inner life of a people. It is the hived-up wisdom, the concentrated light and sweetness, of many generations of men. It is, as has been said by one who is himself a master of literature, " the best thoughts of the best minds through many generations." It is the thought-product of the clearest, most penetrating, and most sympathetic insight of the natures most rarely and richly endowed. It is an account or reflex of the life of a people, not simply of their rulers, political or ecclesiastical; not of the doings of the court or the legislature; not a recital of the great events of war, diplomacy, or finance, but what the people thought and felt and did. Neither is it the expression or picture of the external, physical conditions of the life of the people. You have not given a true account of a man when you have told how high he is, what the color of his hair is, what food he eats, and what kind of a house he lives in.

The deepest and best part of every man's life, and of every nation's life, is inner, silent, invisible. Suppose we could preserve and reproduce with fidelity the material conditions of life exactly as they existed in England, say five hundred years ago. By literature we are enabled to do this for the real, inner, soul-life of a people. Literature is the attempt to express, in one form or another, in history, oration, poem, drama, or fiction, the deep inner life of a great people. There is required for the accomplishment of this task the supreme quality which we describe by the word "genius," and genius is good sense, quick sympathy, patient labor, clear insight, the capacity to think naturally, spontaneously, powerfully, fruitfully. Genius lights its own fires.

The spirit of Christian manliness discloses its presence and power in literature in many ways. It does it, in the first place, by its superiority to the peculiar temptations which present themselves to the qualities of the mind required to create, inspire, and mold a literature. If it be given to those who aspire to create a literature to see farther into the reality of life, the truth of things, than other men, it is also required of them that they truly and faithfully report back what they see. The temptation is always present to bring back a distorted report, or a partial report, or an untrue report, and therein manhood, as it appears in literature and has its battle to fight there, must bring back, must describe what actually exists, and not what an aberrant or eccentric genius thinks should be there. A genuine, honest report from the depths of human life is required of the genius that would assert its claim to manhood in the highest realms of intellectual activity. Manliness in literature must conform to its own high and glowing ideals, and it must give us, not what we indolently wish, but what we clearly need, for our soul's health. It must have the clear insight necessary to discern between the idle want and the spiritual need, and the courage to show us the latter.

Genius must also, in the realm of literature, show itself to be courageous in the presence of difficulties. Genius may find itself poor, but poverty affords no sufficient ground for the flight of genius from its difficult and lonely duties. One may find himself slenderly equipped in this world's goods not only, but his lot and work cast in a political society in which birth and rank and wealth take precedence of capacity, virtue, and worth. But genius, if it be true to the noble ideals of a lofty spiritual manhood, must not yield to these adverse elements, but in all its efforts to describe and paint the thought-life of a people rise gloriously superior to all that is narrowing, cramping, and confining.

Genius in literature, indeed in every realm in which it works, but here especially, must not only acknowledge in general terms the law of moral obligation, but must confess the gradations of that law, its intensification, its increasing stringency, in proportion to the greatness of one's light, opportunity, and gifts. Genius—that is, opulence of intellectual endowment—instead of being an excuse for falseness, cruelty, and immorality, creates additional obligation, multiplies and sharpens the reasons for a higher morality and a purer spirituality on the part of the gifted man. "For unto whomsoever much is given, of him shall much be required."

The three elements heretofore defined as entering into Christian manliness and constituting its very life appear here; namely, courage, dutifulness, love. Following our course on preceding evenings, let us take some practical illustration of what we mean by this. When, in the year 1826, the American writer and scholar, William H. Prescott, found himself in practical possession of the material necessary to write his history of the reign of Ferdinand and Isabella he lost his eyesight, and had no prospect of ever again recovering it. This was a serious discouragement and difficulty, and one apparently insurmountable, but it was not to conquer the man who had consecrated himself to write the history of that great time. He was not appalled; nor was he more than temporarily discouraged. He first hired a reader, and sat in a darkened room listening for hours to a man who knew no modern language but the Spanish; and thus he worked his way through several venerable quartos until he was satisfied of the feasibility of his task. After a time, discharging the reader, he dictated to a more competent man, and worked on as best he could until, by "the

Jesus and the Great Masters of Literature. 57

blessing of Providence," to use his own words, his eyes recovered sufficient strength to allow him to use them, and, by working a limited number of hours each day, he gradually surmounted all these difficulties, and enriched American literature with that delightful and fascinating history. The loss of eyesight by this gifted man only proved to be an occasion for the victorious assertion of the finer and nobler qualities of his character.

William Wordsworth declared that he was not so much called as consecrated; that he was not certain that he had ever made any vows for himself, but he was sure that somebody had made vows for him, and "he felt himself a consecrated spirit." His mission—what did he feel it to be? That he should leave the crowded towns and go to the country, where he could find green grass and hills and lakes and mountains, and live a simple and uncorrupt life; that he should patiently and reverently study his own heart and the hearts of the plain people about him; so living, that he should write simple and natural poetry, and he declared that he had a vocation to do this; that almighty God had consecrated him to that work. When, after some years, he failed to receive any public recognition, and his friends and the members of his family, especially his brothers, were restless because of this lack of appreciation, he said, "Make yourselves at rest concerning me; I speak the truths whose power the world must feel at last." In eight years not a single edition of his early poems could be sold in the English market.

When Cottle, a bookseller in Bristol, conveyed his property to the Messrs. Longman, of London, the only volume marked on the inventory as worth "nil" was a book containing "The Ancient Mariner," by Samuel Taylor Coleridge, and the lines of Wordsworth on "Revisiting Tintern Abbey." He waited, and worked, and thought, and walked by the side of the mountain streamlet, and looked into the open faces of the mountain children, and talked to the peasant in the fields, and watched the procession of the clouds in the sky, and listened to the storm-winds, and kept his soul open to all the voices of God. He educated a generation to appreciate his poetry, and all natural poetry. At last they sent for him at Oxford, and in the ancient theater of that splendid university, in the presence of more than three thousand people, clad in a scarlet robe, Oxford honored itself by conferring upon him its honorary degree. A little later Sir Robert Peel, the Prime Minister of England, extended to him the laureateship of England. What a change since the time when Byron sneered at him, and the *Edinburgh Review* threatened to crush him! He had fought his fight and won his battle, and the world was made to feel the power and reality of the truths he had to utter. He was true to his early and consecrated ideal of life and poetry; he waited, like our own Emerson, for the world to come round to him, instead of running round after the world.

In 1825, Sir Walter Scott was at the height of his splendid fame. He had given to the world his great works of poetry, and had delighted it with his masterpieces of fiction. His farm on the banks of the Tweed, at first scarcely a hundred acres, had grown to be a large estate. The plain dwelling, with its two spare bedrooms, had expanded to the ample proportions of a noble baronial castle. Here he lived in affluence, splendor, joy. In the morning he wrote, not under the spur and lash, not chafed and fretted, but according to the free inspirations of his glorious genius. Then dinner with his friends (and his house was always full of them), and in the afternoon society and recreation. It has been said that no mansion in Europe for so long a term of years so hospitably and graciously entertained so large a number of distinguished guests. In 1826 the printing-house of Ballantyne, in Edinburgh, in which he was largely interested, failed, and it seemed as though he was hopelessly involved. He was humbled before the great world that had so long admired and praised and honored him. He was covered with debt, well-nigh beggared. There were those, versed in the law, who advised him that, by resorting to certain legal stratagems, he could escape the claims of his creditors. See his manhood! He refuses to be dealt with as an ordinary bankrupt. He thrusts aside the legal temptation with noble scorn, not having learned the modern idea of escaping a moral obligation by a legal trick. Hear him: "Give me time, and I will pay all." Then began the fearful struggle. He leaves his invalid wife and his splendid home, goes to Edinburgh, hires small lodgings, and writes to pay his debts. From his fertile brain and unresting hands comes book after book, until in a few years the mountain of debt begins sensibly to diminish. And when at last his brain gave way, and they took him to Italy in the vain hope of restoring his health, in the wanderings of his great mind he still kept murmuring about paying the debt, and after his death it was found that he had worked hard enough to pay every pound of it. Did he die? Do such men really die? Does the blatant infidelity of this time tell me that such men go out in utter oblivion? Is extinction the appointed doom of a great soul like this? Then God is dead, and life is a lie. Such men must master death, or there is no moral order in the universe.

I heartily rejoice that all the stories about the immoral youth of "gentle Will Shakespeare" have at last been exploded, and that he, the greatest of all the writers in our English tongue, has been found at last, by a most eminent authority on English literature, to have lived a dutiful, clean, sweet, wholesome life. Married at eighteen to a woman eight years his senior, at twenty-two years of age his father was threatened with imprisonment for debt; the next year he was arrested, and he who was once a bailiff is now haunted by bailiffs. His father's family was large, and the son had a wife and three children to provide for, so he went up to London for work. At what he worked in the six years that followed his arrival in that city not much is known. This much is known: that he worked his way manfully to the front; that as soon as he began to prosper his father was remembered by having a good allowance settled upon him; that Ann Hathaway and his children were moved to the best house on the main street of Stratford; that William Shakespeare visited them year after year; that he was the first man in the history of English literature ever known to have saved a single cent out of his earnings as an author, and that, having acquired a fair competency, he returned to Stratford to live and die with his wife and children, and father and mother. This is the true record of the private life of the great poet. No man can doubt the moral health of Shakespeare who, with open eye and unprejudiced mind, has studied his writings. Where does he give security to wrong-doing? Does he not in every drama conduct us at last to the triumph of righteousness? Does he not strengthen for us the ethical foundations of life? Where does sin stain as on the pages of Shakespeare? Where is conscience armed with such terrific power? Where is retribution so just, so certain, so overwhelming?

The spirit of Jesus is present in all sound and enduring literature. The spirit of Jesus, I say; not his name, necessarily, nor is it well that it should be. Reverence in literature is no more betokened by the frequent use of the name of Jesus than superior piety is indicated by a constant use of that word in ordinary conversation. Where genuine reverence exists names are sparingly used; but more and more the spirit of Jesus pervades all healthy, wholesome, inspiring literature. How do you detect its presence? Have you ever read a book that distinctly lowered your moral tone? His spirit was not there. Have you ever read an essay, or a poem, or a novel—have you ever read any thing anywhere—that glossed over the eternal distinction between right and wrong? The spirit of Jesus was not in it. Have you ever, after reading a book, risen from it with a cold, a contemptuous and cynical view of man? The spirit of Jesus was not in it. Have you ever read a book that seemed to take all spiritual glow from off the land and the sea, and from the great infinite blue above? The spirit of Jesus was not there, for his presence and spirit consecrate and hallow all things. Have you ever, as the result of your reading, felt that your faith was withering, that the invisible, eternal realities were becoming dim, vague, unreal? The spirit of Jesus was not there. Whenever you have read a book, whether the writer was regular or irregular, pronounced orthodox or heterodox by those who assume to make these distinctions; whenever you have read a book that has made you reverence men and women and children more, deepened your love for liberty and truth and purity, increased your power of moral discrimination, augmented moral energy; whenever you have read a book that made God more real and potent, a present strength and solace, a book that made you strong in the abiding faith that death would not shatter and destroy man, but be to him a translation and a coronation, then you have read a book instinct with the very spirit of Jesus; and this spirit is the life of literature. Where it is absent the literature hastens to decay, where it is present the literature is assured of immortality.

Every great literature has its distinctive characteristics. If a people be dreamy, subtle, patient, contemplative, their literature will partake of these elements. Such is the character of the Hindu mind, and such is the character of the Hindu literature. If a people be light, airy, gay, given to pleasure, their literature will be light, airy, gay, and it will apotheosize pleasure. The French people are such a people, and the French people have produced such a literature. If a people be reflective, given to inquiry into the reason of things, acute, penetrating, painstaking, philosophic, then you will find a solid, massive literature, dealing with the greatest problems in the most earnest, thorough, and reverent way. Such a people are the Germans, and such is the literature of the Fatherland. The distinctive characteristic of English literature is its moral vigor, its moral sanity, its moral wholesomeness and sweetness. There are spots on the sun, but that which marks off the English from all other literatures is its sense of duty to be done. It is not deficient in other qualities. In fancy, in satire and wit, in fire and energy and strength, in boldness of imagination, in passion and pathos, in splendor and majesty of expression, in a certain lofty, resounding eloquence, it is a literature worthy of the immortality to which it seems destined. These qualities, however, do not constitute its peculiar power, its crowning glory. The true glory of the literature of England has been well expressed by one who says that it "represents a people striving through successive generations to find out the right and do it, to root out the wrong, and labor ever onward for the love of God." The English still believe, and have always believed, that to fear God and keep his commandments was the whole duty of man. Hence the moral robustness of their literature; hence their hatred of wrong and injustice, and their noble devotion to liberty and law.

Their earliest poet, Cædmon, had the fear of God before his eyes, and sang of God, and of duty to God, in the first great English hymn. The sweet and gentle Aldhelm, as early as the seventh century, testified to the English sense of duty by taking his stand on the bridge between the town and country, and singing a song to keep the people from running home from church directly after mass, without waiting for the sermon. The Venerable Bede, the first of English prose writers, died praying, and dictating to one of his students a new translation of the gospel of John into English. The wise and good King Alfred, by his translation of the *Consolations of Boethius*, confessed that we men need inward strengthening as well as outward comfort. The scene of the *Decameron* of Boccaccio is laid in a beautiful garden, not far from the plague-stricken city of Florence, and his characters while away the time by telling witty and disgusting stories while their friends are smitten with the plague. That is, his characters are represented as running away from their duty. The pilgrims of Chaucer's *Canterbury Tales* are on their way to the shrine of Thomas à Becket, and, with their light in that age, that to them was a service of duty. The *Utopia* of Sir Thomas More was a dream of moral excellence and spiritual beauty, rather than of physical comfort and political progress. In his songs and his romance of *Arcadia*, in his life and in his death, Sir Philip Sidney acknowledged and obeyed the high behests of duty. The *Faery Queen* of Spenser is simply a magnificent poetic exaltation of holiness, justice, chastity, temperance, and friendship. Where, in all literature, is there any thing comparable with Shakespeare's awful descriptions of the power of an awakened conscience? In the guilty terror of Macbeth, in the sleep-walking of Lady Macbeth, in the ghosts that troubled the dreams of Richard the night before the battle of Bosworth Field, and bid him despair and die, in the baffled prayer of Claudius, in the tragic revenge of Hamlet, in all his mighty dramas, the lesson is ever the same:

"Be just and fear not:
Let all the ends thou aimest at be thy country's,
Thy God's, and truth's; then, if thou fall'st,
Thou fall'st a blessed martyr."

There is no sickly sentiment in Shakespeare. The wrong-doer hastens on to an inevitable and awful fate. There is no safety but in righteousness. Milton's whole life was a noble psalm of duty, and every line he wrote testifies to his loyalty to the highest right he knew. When old and poor and blind and deserted, he did not " bate a jot of heart or hope," but he still bore up, and steered right onward. The purity of Addison's style is equaled by the purity of his heart, and the delicacy of his wit is surpassed by the delicacy of his moral perceptions. Old Dr. Johnson was perpetually teaching that men must do right if they would be happy. The poetry of Wordsworth has for its chief end the exaltation of the humble duties of every-day life and work. Macaulay does not allow his admiration for Bacon, the philosopher, to obscure his perception of the moral obliquity of Bacon, the judge. Wrong is wrong, even if Bacon commits it. Tennyson sings to the men who are doubters to-day that it is only by unfaltering devotion to duty that they may hope to enter into light and peace. To hate falseness, to fight shams, to get the evil out of our hearts and out of the world, to be true, honest, faithful, earnest, sincere—this is the teaching and preaching of the much-misunderstood sage of Chelsea. A sense of God, of our capacity to know him, of our ability to obey him, of our happiness if we do so, of our misery if we follow the devices of our own hearts, in short, the supremacy of conscience, the sovereignty of duty—this it is which has made the English people great and the English literature immortal.

American literature is not unworthy of its high

descent. It, too, sings the songs of duty and right.
Its voice is not that of a siren. It charms to invigorate and strengthen, not to debilitate and destroy.
It is full of moral vigor and health. It is clean,
wholesome, inspiring. Its masters have ever been
the servants, not the hirelings, of truth. Whittier
and Longfellow and Holmes and Bryant and Hawthorne and Emerson and Prescott and Irving and
Lowell and Curtis and Holland have all the same
lesson to teach—we must obey God if we would become and remain strong, wise, and free. I covet
for the creators and guides of our literature all rare
gifts of genius, all wealth of fancy, all wisdom of
thought, all fire of eloquence, all felicity of expression, but chiefly do I pray that they, and all writers
every-where, may never fail to teach that wrong at
last shall be overtaken and punished, and right
shall be eternally triumphant. The ultimate sovereignty in literature belongs to manhood!

GREAT MEN IN HISTORY.

For all that is in the world, the lust of the flesh, and the lust of the eyes, and the pride of life, is not of the Father, but is of the world. And the world passeth away, and the lust thereof: but he that doeth the will of God abideth forever.—1 John ii, 16, 17.

THE history of man on this globe has hitherto been largely that of an animal; he has lived in the realm of the present, the physical, the seen, and the temporal. The immediate, not the remote, the present, not the future, that which solicits him now, the food that his eyes, and his ears, and his mouth, and his stomach crave—these things, and not the opening up, the enrichment, and the satisfaction of his reasoning faculties, his moral sentiments, and his spiritual capacities; the things that are present, palpable, physical—food, lands, dress, houses, money, empire—in these elements, and along these lines, man has hitherto been largely content to have his life. It is a sad reflection that the majority of men live in that realm still. I am not a phrenologist, certainly not a practical phrenologist, but I see many men whose heads and necks greatly belie them if they are not thralled by the physical and animal elements of their natures; many men in whom "the lust of the flesh, and the lust of the eyes, and the pride of life" make up the whole existence. How narrow, dwarfed, shriveled is the spirit-life of most men! There is reason to fear that many so-called religious people, stripped of all their present secular activities and physical enjoyments, would find themselves at a loss for congenial occupation. What would you do if you did not have to make your bread and butter? How would you spend your time? In what direction would your energies seek vent? Suppose you did not have to work ten or twelve hours to-morrow, what would you do? When men sit down seriously to reflect upon how short the distance is that measures the length of our journey away from the animal, it is rather a sobering thought. Consider this one fact: that the most glittering prizes of the most enlightened and civilized states of the Christian world are still given to great soldiers. France gave the best she had to Napoleon; there was nothing England had which she withheld from Wellington; there was nothing that we had which we withheld from Grant; we were on the very verge of violating the unwritten tradition against a third term, in order to heap still greater honors upon him. A great soldier (stripped of all honeyed phraseology) means a man who has been pre-eminently successful in killing his fellow-men. Of course we disguise it by fine talk about liberty and progress, and self-defense as the first law of nature, and a great many other high-sounding phrases, but, stripped of all these thin veils and outer wrappings, a great soldier simply means the man who can most successfully kill in the shortest possible time the greatest number of his fellow-men; and that kind of a man has within his grasp the most solid, splendid, and enduring guerdons which may be bestowed upon him by the most highly civilized states. It is as Gibbon has said, in substance, in his *Decline and Fall of the Roman Empire*, the destroyers of mankind have been esteemed its greatest benefactors, and have received its greatest honors.

How great a part cunning has played in the world! In recent times we have called it "diplomacy," but diplomacy for thousands of years meant a match game of cunning: the greatest deceiver, the man who could tell the biggest and most plausible lie and make it to appear so like the truth as to ensnare his antagonist was the best diplomatist. Diplomacy for many centuries was simply a game of cunning, and the man who was the most foxy won the victory.

What a part greed has played in the world! By greed I mean covetousness; an inordinate and consuming desire for wealth. How strong is the passion for possession! The "yellow" fever, how it has burned in the veins of men! The greatest peril of the republic at this hour springs from the selfish and corrupt use of money. The United States Senate is very rapidly becoming a plutocratic body. I do not know how many Senators are there now who are supposed to represent the various Pacific railroads. We read of men representing this railroad and that railroad, this corporation and that corporation, this important interest and the other important interest; and if the Legislatures should select another group of senators such as they have elected for a number of years, we shall have made our Senate a plutocratic body—a body of patricians, founded not upon blood, not upon brains, not upon character, but upon the power of "money in politics." Consider how much a lucrative office in New York costs, according to the testimony of the men who are familiar with the "assessments" made upon candidates by the various "halls" and "bosses" who control this great city. Go back three thousand years, before there had been given to the world any of the refining and spiritualizing influences which spring from a pure Christianity, and what must the great soldier have been then? Is it any wonder that men bowed down and worshiped him and made him a god? We almost do it now. Is it any wonder that in those early times the strong or the cunning man ruled the tribe? Is it any wonder that wealth had such corrupting and debauching power?

Have you ever remarked how potent was the influence of commanding talent or genius, without any regard to its moral character? We may admire the work of the men who have made the canvas breathe, and the marble speak, and the flowing numbers entrance the nations, but it will not always do to look too closely into their lives. Not seldom their rank offenses have smelt to heaven. Jesus said, "the first shall be last, and the last shall be first." I recall a circumstance which deeply impressed this truth on my mind. I was called to the funeral of a godly woman, one who had lived a modest, humble, dutiful life. There was nothing in the morning papers about her life or death. There was something in them as to who should be Marshal of northern Alabama; there was a good deal on district representation; there was a good deal about where the next National Democratic Convention should be held; there was the usual full account of burglaries, defalcations, divorces, and murders; but, of course, not one word about this woman's life of toil and duty and beauty. A good many years ago she found herself with five boys, the oldest not twelve years, the youngest sixteen days old, face to face with the world, in poverty to feed and clothe them, to teach them the lessons of truth, purity, and wisdom. It was a long and severe struggle, away from the world's applauding eye, but she did her work well. As I sat in the ferry-boat, I did not see any public building draped in mourning; I heard neither boom of cannon nor roll of drum; I beheld no external indication that this brave and earnest life had come to an end. And yet she succeeded; her life was a glorious success. When is a life a success? When we do well what God sent us here to do. Garfield succeeded when General Buell sent him with twenty-five hundred men into south-western Kentucky, to drive out Humphrey Marshall with five thousand. He did the work he had been sent to do, and they made him a brigadier-general. This woman did what God had appointed her to do, and by so doing she glorified him on the earth, and is now gone to enjoy him forever. Do you suppose there is any record up there of who got the appointment for marshal in northern Alabama? Do you suppose there is any record up there about district representation? Do you suppose there is any record up there of the proposed horizontal reduction of the tariff? Do you suppose there is any record up there of nine tenths of all you read in the daily papers every morning? But what this woman did is recorded there. When the solemn reversals of eternity shall even up the hard inequalities of this time, it will be found that often the last here are the first here, and the first here are the last there.

Has Christian manliness never been triumphant in history? Have those qualities in human nature that we have hitherto tried to group and descrieb under the three words, courage, dutifulness, love, never won supreme victory in the history of the race? What was the secret of the power of Columbus? His great and pure character! What was it in Martin Luther that overawed the splendid assembly at Worms? It was the downright integrity of the man, his simple and sublime faith in, and loyalty to, the right. "Here stand I; I can do no other. God help me." And was he not making history? This it was which ennobled and glorified John Bunyan, and strengthened him to say, after an incarceration of twelve years, "I have determined yet to suffer, the Almighty God being my helper, even until the moss shall grow over my eyebrows, if frail life shall continue so long, rather than violate my faith and my principles." He was a history-maker. And so was honest Hugh Latimer, not only when preaching at Paul's Cross, but when he bade Master Ridley to be of good cheer and play the man. This was the real secret of the fiery eloquence, electric and contagious, of Wendell Phillips, one of the great makers of our history. He was a patrician, but that will be forgotten; he was a scholar, but that will be forgotten; he was the greatest orator of the English-speaking races of his time, but that will pale into a dim tradition; but while the memory of mankind endures it will never be forgotten that the patrician, the scholar, the orator ostracized himself for a poor, despised, enslaved race, facing in the center of culture in America the rage and fury of the "broadcloth mob," and that throughout his whole life he had the unerring sagacity to pierce through all external disguises and wrappings, and see the right, and, seeing it, he had the courage to bow himself down to it, and the faith to know that in so doing he served God.

This is manhood in history! and when a whole crowd of the petty names now being dinned into our ears are lost in the rubbish of the ages, the brave and eloquent patrician-commoner of New England, Wendell Phillips, will be remembered with gratitude, with respect, with ever-increasing and imperishable honor. "The memory of the wicked shall rot, but the righteous shall be had in everlasting remembrance."

When I was a boy, beginning to read a little, the

name of Socrates, the old Greek, used to puzzle me greatly. I could not find out what he had ever done; I could not find out that he had ever built any city, that he had ever commanded any armies, that he had ever devised any system of finance, that he had ever rescued the state by any comprehensive measure of statesmanship. And yet he has won a unique and commanding place in the history of the race, and men every-where unite to do honor to his name. Now, by what forces, by the concurrence of what influences, was he lifted to this high, serene, and ample place? Why should we call him the greatest and wisest of the Greeks? He was not the mythical founder of a great state, as Numa or Theseus; he was not an original law-giver, as Solon or Lycurgus; he was not a genius in statesmanship, as was Pericles; he was not a victorious general, as was Miltiades; he rescued no oppressed cities, as did Timoleon; he built no splendid temples and carved no great statues of the immortal gods, as did the great Phidias; he did not aspire to the distinction of a poet-philosopher, as did his illustrious disciple, the divine Plato. Nevertheless, he is greater than any of them, more widely known than any other Greek. Put it to the test of the average unlettered man on the street, and while he has heard of Socrates he knows nothing of Miltiades, or Pericles, or Timoleon, or Phidias. Why? He became one of the ruling forces in history solely by virtue of the supremacy in him of ethical manhood. He was a sound man at the core. The root of the matter was in him—righteousness. He is not, indeed, to be judged by his country and his age; his moral rule suffers by comparison with ours; he was not a perfect character; we are not to forget that he was an Athenian of pre-Christian times; but as far as it was given him to see the light he courageously and steadfastly followed it, utterly regardless of consequences. He talked about a "demon" that went about with him, and whenever this demon, or voice, or divine intimation told him not to do any thing he would not do it; and it so happened that this demon, or voice, or divine intimation generally told him not to do things that were wrong. His manhood was exhibited in the winter campaign at Potidæa, where the rigors of the northern climate of Thrace could not chill his spirits nor freeze his patriotism. It shone forth illustriously in his bold and perilous rescue of his friend Xenophon, amid the confusion and flight that followed the defeat at Delium. He never held office but once in his life, and then but for a single day; that was quite long enough for the fickle and venal Athenians to have such a man as Socrates in office. Athens had been engaged in an unsuccessful war, and certain rivals of the ten generals commanding the Athenian armies were stirring up the people against them to demand their execution. It so happened that in regular turn, going around among the tribes, the lot fell to Socrates to preside that day. The measure was illegal in form and iniquitous in substance, and so he nobly refused to put it to vote. They tried every art known to wily and supple Greeks in order to swerve him from the right; they threatened him, they flattered him, they entreated him, they denounced him; but the ugly old man stood there all day and quietly and calmly and persistently and inflexibly refused to put the question to vote. He was never again called to the discharge of any public trust in Athens, and I doubt if to-day he could be elected to Congress in America! On the day of his trial, when he stood in the presence of his superstitious and unjust judges, he used this memorable language: "Men of Athens, I honor and love you; but I shall obey the gods rather than you, and while I have life and health I shall never cease from the practice and teaching of virtue, exhorting any one whom I meet after my manner, and convincing him, saying, 'O my friend, why do you, who are a citizen of the great and mighty and wise city of Athens, care so much about laying up the greatest amount of money and honor and reputation, and so little about wisdom and truth and the greatest improvement of the soul, which you never regard or heed at all?'" When they found him guilty, hoping to escape the infliction of a capital sentence, they turned to him and asked him what the sentence should be; and the old man, seventy years of age, with biting sarcasm, answered, "I suppose I ought to be maintained in honor at the expense of the State for the remainder of my life as a reward for my eminent services thereto." Then they took another vote and sentenced him to death. During the absence of the sacred vessel at Delos, it was unlawful for the Athenians to execute a capital sentence. His friends thought to improve this opportunity to secure his escape. They bribed the jailer, they secured a swift-flying trireme, they provided a secure retreat in Thessaly, and then, acquainting him with their plans, they urged him to fly. He declared that he had devoted all his life to teaching the duty of obedience to the laws, and that he would not now furnish a public example of disobedience. They tell him that he has been unlawfully condemned. He replies that wrong never justifies wrong. His virtue is proof alike against the malice of his enemies and the entreaties of his friends.

How memorable is that death-scene in Athens! In pathetic interest and moral sublimity there is but one greater in the whole history of mankind. What a strange glory surrounds that last day in prison! He spent his final hours in conversation with his friends on the relation of pain and pleasure, on the cowardice of suicide, on the nature of virtue, on the immortality of the soul. In the midst of their pleasant converse the hour of doom arrives. The executioner reluctantly approaches him, holding in his hand the cup of hemlock, and tells him that the hour has come, and then burst into tears. Socrates held it for a moment, and said: "Is there enough to secure the purpose for which it was appointed, and also to permit me to make a libation to the gods?" And he was answered in the negative. He then asked for directions, and, having received them, he composedly drank the fatal potion at one draught, without a single change of feature. The long pent-up emotion of his friends bursts forth in loud weeping, but he gently chides them, reminding them that he had sent the women away hours before that he might have a quiet and peaceful death. He walked around the room until he felt the languor was in his limbs, and then lying down upon his couch he covered his face. Gradually the torpor reached his heart. The hour of his departure is at hand, and while the golden sunlight yet lingers on the hills that guard the City of the Violet Crown the spirit of Socrates goes to join the invisible assembly of the pure and the good, and to mingle forever with the spirits of just men made perfect. He was not a great poet, as Homer; he was not a great orator, as Demosthenes; he was not a great dramatist, as Sophocles; he was not a great king, as Xerxes; he was not a great general, as Hannibal; he was not a great statesman, as Cæsar; he was not a maker of systems, as Aristotle; he restored no cities, as Themistocles; but he was a man great enough, noble enough, honest enough, to see the simple and universal truth, and abide by it, that he who fears God and works righteousness has exhausted the whole meaning of human life. The glory of Athens has departed; "her freedom and her power have for more than twenty centuries been annihilated; her people have degenerated into timid slaves, her language into a barbarous jargon; her temples have been given up to the successive depredations of Romans, Turks, and Scotchmen;" the unrivaled splendors of her Acropolis, gleaming far out to guide the returning mariner to the city of his passionate love, have faded and perished; but the name of Socrates, like a glowing star, shines with increasing luster and brilliancy across the wide and solemn spaces of the centuries. In the long roll of the ages, his is the only name that Christian men have ever ventured to compare with the Name that is above every name.

This truth is susceptible of a broader application; it will bear, and it demands, an application to nations. Manhood in history is most conspicuously illustrated in the causes that have governed the rise, growth, and decay of nations. It is that particular period in the history of a nation when the balance swings over from righteousness to falseness, dishonesty, cowardice, cruelty, sensuality, and baseness that the causes begin to operate which in their final issue decide its ultimate overthrow. In the earlier periods of the history of the Greek race their false religion held them fast at least to the common fundamental virtues; but when the era of overflowing wealth and leisure and luxury and skepticism set in, and when at last the Greeks would have changed our formula—Courage, dutifulness, love—and would have said, "Gold, beauty, intellect"—then Greece was gone, and nothing could rescue her. When she tried to purchase her safety by distributing gold to Philip of Macedon, when she pretended that duty could be transformed into beauty, when in her swelling intellectual vanity she believed that if the gods were to come to the earth they would speak in the language of Plato, then the fate of Greece was sealed. In the early history of Rome no nation or people could long stand before her; but when wealth accumulated, when, finally, instead of dutifulness there came undutifulness and disobedience, when the Roman husband asserted and exercised the right of free divorce from his wife, the right to put her away at his will, when the time came that they held such banquets in the houses of the wealthy as you may see portrayed in a striking painting now in the Metropolitan Museum of Art, when, to protect themselves from mob violence, they threw largesses of wheat to the half-starving populace, the very heart of manhood in Rome was eaten out, and the time had come for the Goths and Vandals to portion her off. Wheresoever the carcass is, the birds of prey are gathered together.

There is a modern nation that has attempted more than once to build itself on something else than truth, virtue, and holiness, seeking some artificial substitute for personal righteousness. I would not do injustice to France, but, if I read her history aright, her formula for nearly a hundred years has too often been "Glory, pleasure, passion," and she has attempted by that formula to lead the world. What has been the result? She has gone down again and again before sturdier peoples, and I have no faith in the permanence of the present republic unless the French people fall in love with sober, self-renouncing virtue; unless the French people learn that courage, dutifulness, love—not glory, pleasure, passion—constitute the strength of a great nation.

With all the faults and sins of England, she has endured for twelve glorious centuries, and where is the nation that can conquer her now? Why? Because the body of her people are and have always been sound at heart. And America—we are in no danger so long as the body of the people are sound. I have not much hope when I take an afternoon stroll on Broadway and Fifth Avenue, and look upon these gilded youths, with their mutton-chop whiskers, and their hair parted in the middle, or banged low on the forehead, the light fringe of down on their upper lips, oiled and perfumed, their pants fitting like gloves, and their tooth-pick shoes—my hope of this country is not built upon such manikins as these; but because I believe the great body of the people to be uncorrupted, because I know that all over this land the majority of plain, sincere, home-loving people still believe in courage, dutifulness, love, I do firmly believe that we will weather many a future storm, and that if we continue to keep sound at heart we will weather all storms.

Jesus came to supereminent personal power and influence. All other names pale their ineffectual fires before his name. We think not of Socrates or Confucius, of Zoroaster or Buddha, or any man of ancient or modern times in his serene and superior presence. What were the forces, what the elements, what the conditions of the strange and marvelous power to which the Nazarene has come? Our fathers in theology and apologetics honestly thought that the best method of proving the great power of Jesus was by assuming the truth of the miracles, and then arguing that whoever could work such miracles must necessarily be divine. We have learned a more natural and convincing way. We take him in his inherent and essential and indestructible moral glory and perfection, without break or flaw or fault, and we say that the greater miracle of his sinlessness must include the lesser miracles ascribed to his power. Socrates is demonstrably defective; Jesus Christ is absolutely faultless. In this he is unique. Here he stands alone. I know of no other being in whose behalf the claim is raised that he was absolutely sinless. How did he come to this power? Not by writing books; he never wrote any books, he never led any armies, he never founded any state, he never created a literature, he never established a philosophy, he was not the head of a school of art; he moved among the people in Palestine quietly and simply, and declared that his Father had sent him into this world to do his will, and he offered no other reason for his being here. This was his message concerning himself: "I am here to do my Father's will;" and he went about doing it, quietly, simply, faithfully, lovingly, and he did it to the end. The power of Jesus is the power of absolute righteousness.

My friends, let us not be deceived, GOD is not mocked. Whatsoever a man soweth, that shall he also reap; whatsoever a nation soweth, that also shall it reap. No man can build on falseness and gather the fruits of honesty; no man can build on unrighteousness and gather the fruits of righteousness. Be sure your sin will find you out. Righteousness is safe, righteousness is profitable, righteousness is the power of Jesus Christ, righteousness is the will of Almighty God. "The world passeth away, and the lust thereof; but he that doeth the will of God abideth forever."

CHRISTIAN MANLINESS IN TRIAL.

From that time many of his disciples went back, and walked no more with him. Then said Jesus unto the twelve, Will ye also go away? Then Simon Peter answered him, Lord, to whom shall we go? thou hast the words of eternal life. And we believe and are sure that thou art that Christ, the Son of the living God.—John vi, 66–69.

I AM to speak to you to-night on Christian Manliness in Trial. Manliness is tried or put to the test in all those experiences and conditions of human life which menace the steadfastness, the unselfishness, the heroism of our virtues. Who is there with sufficient hardihood to undertake an exhaustive catalogue of such experiences and conditions? In short, this is a probationary state of being, this whole life is a trial life, this time is a testing time, and our environment is what it is for the fulfillment of the final, gracious purposes of Almighty God.

The problem of human existence on this globe resolves itself at last to this: the evolution, under divine superintendence and care, of perfect spiritual beings by the mysterious ministry of growth, struggle, and trial. Sickness, pain, the gradual approach of certain death—in such experiences Christian manliness is put to the trial. Manliness is tested by poverty and by wealth, by obscurity and by fame, by defeat and by success, by failure and by victory. Calumny, public vituperation and abuse, secret solicitation to evil, devotion to unpalatable truth, the service, in the presence of a hostile public opinion, of the despised and degraded classes in society, loneliness, the irreducible inequalities of society, betrayal, the seeming strength of wickedness, the seeming weakness of righteousness —these words imperfectly denote some of the conditions by which our manliness is here tested.

How easy it is for a man to secure a cheap, ephemeral reputation by the vigorous and courageous denunciation of dead or dying errors! To illustrate my thought, how cheap it is to-day for a Protestant preacher to denounce the errors of Roman Catholicism! How easy it is for him to array himself against its dead or dying errors in the presence of a sympathetic audience, who will be sure, at least inwardly, to applaud. Every bigot and zealot present will be especially delighted. How brave it is to get a reputation as a Defender of the Faith when perhaps there is not a Catholic present, and if there should be one, and he should rise and undertake a defense of his faith, he would be cast out of the synagogue! Now, this is not the spirit of the men who three hundred years ago denounced Catholicism. The men of that day were face to face with Catholicism in its living power, and for them to denounce its errors probably meant, and in very many instances actually meant, imprisonment, social ostracism, the fagot, death in some cruel form. But it is not manly to seek to obtain a temporary reputation by the vigorous and unsparing denunciation of error that is either dead or in the last gasp. I put this in that I might preach a little to myself. I have preached a good deal to you, and it is well sometimes for the preacher to do as the physician does when he comes to our houses—taste his own medicine.

Have you ever heard of the tests to which the manhood of Wellington was submitted in the Peninsular Campaigns? How when he went there he found himself in the presence of 350,000 French soldiers, thirsting for glory and hitherto victorious on almost every battle-field, and led by some of Napoleon's most distinguished marshals, while Wellington had but 30,000 British troops? This was the case for four years, and he was subjected to the test of waiting with 30,000 men in Portugal until by his inactivity the French army should be demoralized, and he raise up a Portuguese and Spanish contingent that would enable him to have the victory. To wait four years at the head of 30,000 men with England clamoring for an attack, and all this time to be unmurmuring, and to abide by his policy until the day for victory came, was the exhibition of a noble manhood.

Nor was this all. One of Napoleon's marshals, when he marched out of Spain, carried with him some of the most valuable pictures in that country. The Duke of Wellington carried out of Spain and Portugal not a cent's worth of any thing that belonged to another man. When he at last crossed the French frontier and news was brought to him that 40,000 Spanish infantry were about to gather fortunes by indiscriminate pillage, he remonstrated with their officers, and when they would not listen to him he sent the whole army back to Spain. At home they were plotting against him; every jealous rival was seeking to undermine him. The home administration at that time was weak, hesitating, dilatory, and not equal to the great emergency; the Spaniards were grasping and rapacious, the Portuguese were ambitious and self-seeking; and yet in the presence of all these difficulties he built up an army, and trained it, and gave it a splendid *esprit du corps*, and at last hurled it against this hitherto victorious French army, and comes down to us the great victor of the Peninsular Campaign. In the midst of his victories he writes a secret letter to the home government: "I am overwhelmed with debt (not his own personal debts, but debts contracted in the prosecution of his campaigns), and can scarcely go out of my house on account of public creditors waiting to demand of me their just dues." Yet he was patient, and waited, and kept himself submissive, and at last, at Waterloo, it was given to this Iron Duke to break forever the power of the most unprincipled political and military adventurer that has ever appeared in the whole history of man.

"Such was he; his work is done.
But while the races of mankind endure
Let his great example stand
Colossal, seen of every land,
And keep the soldier firm, the statesman pure;

Christian Manliness in Trial.

Till in all lands and thro' all human story
The path of duty be the way to glory!"

We think that General Grant was the first American soldier who has been abused. We think that Samuel J. Tilden is the first great public man who has ever had enough patience never to reply to his infamous detractors. We forget that George Washington was scandalously abused and vilified. His manhood was most severely tested in the winter of 1777-78. In the fall of the preceding year Washington had been well-nigh uniformly unsuccessful, while Stark and Gates had been successful. That was the famous winter of Valley Forge. The army was inactive, and the country was impatient. Cabal after cabal was formed against him, and who do you suppose the intriguers were? Leading officers in the Continental army, prominent members of the Continental Congress, and eminent civilians. Forged letters were printed in the newspapers of New York and London, with the avowed purpose of showing that George Washington was insincere in his devotion to the cause of the revolution. His friends besought him to reply, but he nobly refused. Why? Because he could not defend himself without sacrificing the cause. He said to them: "How can I defend myself by a letter? Look at these soldiers. Do they ask me why I am inactive? Shall I reply that the soldiers are almost starved, with insufficient clothing, weakened by exposure? I will wait and see the end." He never wrote a line to defend himself through all that terrible winter. He waited, and worked, and won; and now that the mists have cleared away, yonder he stands, the grandest figure that ever presided over the birth of a great people, the Father of his country: first in war, first in peace, and first in the hearts of his countrymen.

John Milton, loving as he did the "still air of delightful studies," consecrated himself with the fervor and devotion of a religious devotee to the war against the divine right of kings and of tyrannical prelacy in England, and during the struggles of the Long Parliament, and during the Protectorate of Oliver Cromwell, he worked with such uncommon assiduity that at last he became blind. After a while the Commonwealth perished, and the cause seemed lost. Milton was an old man. His daughters cheated him in the market money. An enterprising and generous publisher gave him $25 for the copyright of *Paradise Lost*.

The time came to receive Charles the Second, and reinstate him on the throne of his ancestors, and the people lined the cliffs of Dover and took off their hats and waved them and made the welkin ring with their loud huzzas, but John Milton was not there. If he had been, he would have kept his hat on his head; for he was no obsequious sycophant. He had never learned to "crook the pregnant hinges of the knee, that thrift might follow fawning." He was still a Puritan; no more believing now than twenty years before in prelacy, or the divine right of kings. He never compromised, and in his blind old age, deserted, hated, proscribed, poverty-stricken, he stood by his principles, and pathetically described his situation in one of the noblest tragic dramas in the English language.

And was he complaining? Did he lose faith in Providence? Did he murmur? Listen to his noblest sonnet:

> "Cyriac, this three years day these eyes, though clear
> To outward view of blemish or of spot,
> Bereft of light their seeing have forgot;
> Nor to their idle orbs doth sight appear
> Of sun, or moon, or star, throughout the year,
> Or man or woman. Yet I argue not
> Against Heaven's hand or will, nor bate a jot
> Of heart or hope; but still bear up and steer
> Right onward. What supports me, dost thou ask?
> The conscience, Friend, to have lost them overplied
> In Liberty's defense; my noble task
> Of which all Europe rings from side to side.
> This thought might lead me thro' the world's vain mask,
> Content, though blind, had I no better guide."

It is related that Charles II. and the Duke of York once visited the old man in his humble lodgings to revile him for the part he had taken in the Commonwealth, and that they taunted him on account of the failure of his cause, declaring that he had been justly forsaken of God and man. Charles II., one of the most unscrupulous and dissolute libertines that ever disgraced a throne in the whole history of the world, and the Duke of York, afterward his successor, a narrow, sullen, obstinate bigot —what men to revile Milton! They were the kings then, but Milton is the king now; a king not alone by virtue of his splendid and immortal genius, but quite as much by his devotion to unpopular truth, by his vast and his incalculable services to popular liberty, by the rare purity of his character, and by his deep and calm faith in God and the eternal power of goodness.

On that dreadful, awful, fatal second of July morning, when Garfield was stretched on the floor at Washington City in the public railway station, the sudden shock, the prospect of immediate death, could not unman him; he was equal to the solemn hour, he had no preparation to make—he had made it long ago. When they took him to his room and told him that he had one chance in a hundred, he cheerily replied, " Well, we will take that chance and fight it out." And then for eighty days and nights he looked into the open grave, and he saw all the high ambitions that he had cherished depart one after another, and the weary days and the long nights of pain followed each other, and these things did not break his spirit. His manhood, tested by a sudden shock, was equal to the occasion. His manhood, tested by prolonged and almost unparalleled suffering, was equal to the occasion. Manhood is indeed sovereign over " the undiscovered mystery of pain."

But the great army of unrecorded, unrecognized, unrequited heroes! How many men there have been who in humble places have maintained their manhood unsullied, incorrupt, sound, and whole! An officer in a bank, in a subordinate position, not the president, not the cashier, not striving for the place of president or cashier, calls the attention of a number of the trustees to a system of entries being pursued which were fraudulent in their nature. He again and again pointed out the danger of such entries, and the directors, trying to avoid trouble, not wishing to make any change in the chief officers, accepted his resignation, and for years he found no place until the earnings of his life were gradually exhausted. He was not a distinguished man. His name is not written anywhere in any of the public places of earth. If it is not written yonder, then no book of remembrance is kept.

A young man finds himself with the fatal cough that betokens certain death. He has graduated with honor, he has been admitted to the bar, his prospects in life are unusually flattering, but never to father or mother, never to brother or sister, never to the most intimate friend did he allow one word of complaint or murmuring to escape him as he walked to the grave. Nay, more; within a month of his death, in the full possession of his reason, after much earnest thought, he chose a form of religious faith deemed deadly heresy by his own friends, and was received into a Church that was to them a dangerously heretical Church, and all this he did quietly, and with great respect and love for those whose faith differed so widely from his own. That was heroism.

Have you never heard of Thomas Wright, of Manchester, the foundryman who received not quite $500 a year, and by accident discovered that liberated convicts had a hard time to get an honest place? This honest, brotherly foundryman took these convicts and got them places, and he apportioned his scanty earnings in such a way that a certain sum would be at his disposal temporarily to assist the released convicts for whom he could not find places. He worked in the foundry from six in the morning till six in the evening. In ten years he had secured places for three hundred convicts, all of whom proved themselves trustworthy, and were thus rescued from villainy. Now, do you think that man's name isn't in heaven? When they call the roll in heaven, kings and philosophers and poets and statesmen, popes and cardinals and bishops, a great number of them, must wait until plain Thomas Wright gets his crown.

The beginning of the public ministry of Jesus has been styled a "Galilean spring-time." The music of love that marked the beginning of that ministry was disturbed by but a single discordant note, his rejection by his fellow-townsmen of Nazareth. But at the wedding in Cana of Galilee, in the great crowds that thronged him in the vicinity of Capernaum, Tiberius, and Bethsaida, in the popularity that led him to seek retreat from the crowds at night and early in the morning, that he might have time for prayer and rest, we see how bright and promising in the beginning was the ministry of Jesus.

It is apparent, to those who study the New Testament faithfully, that at the beginning the Pharisees hoped to be able to make use of him as a popular leader. The people were his friends; there was no open break yet with the national Church, no open break with the recognized religious leaders of the nation. Time went on, and first of all his own relatives broke from him, and said that he was beside himself. The first sinister rumor was that he had gone crazy as the result of his enthusiasm for humanity. Then the Pharisees conspired against him, and after a while the Jewish rationalists, the Sadducees, and then the astute, superserviceable politicians of the day, the Herodians, men who were hangers-on in Herod's court, waiting for offices.

Have you ever thought of the epithets applied to Jesus? Sometimes when I read in the papers an unusually abusive and scurrilous article on some worthy public man, I take a piece of paper and write out the epithets that were employed against Jesus. They called him a glutton, a wine-bibber, a heretic, a crazy man, a Sabbath-breaker, a seditionist, and they brought a charge that he was in league with the prince of the devils, a heathen god of such a character that if I should attempt here to describe his filthiness this congregation would not wait to hear the recital; and yet they said that it was by his alliance with Beelzebub, the prince of the devils, that he cast out devils. The people soon fell away from him, and he was left alone. And so Jesus knew what it was to have his manliness tested in trial. "From that time many of his disciples went back, and walked no more with him." Is there any thing more pathetic in the language of man than the words of Jesus at this time to the twelve: "Will ye also go away?" If there is any thing that touches a deeper chord in the being of a reverent man, it is the other question of Jesus to the three disciples in the garden: "What, could ye not watch with me one hour?" So it was that as a Son he was made perfect by suffering.

I summon you to these ranks. I summon you especially, young men, to the manhood that asks, not " How much can this world give me," not " How many friends can I make who will bring wealth and honor to me," but to a loftier type of manliness; to the courage that will lead you to speak the needed but unpalatable truth, to the faith that will inspire you to join the right but unpopular side, to such quiet steadiness of dutifulness as would lead you in an obscure position to do what Thomas Wright, the English foundryman, did.

I call you to be subject to the abuse, to the vituperation, to the slander of the time. I call you to the larger, nobler, diviner life that gives, gives, gives, and is yet glad, smiling, trustful, and brotherly.

I call you to-night to such arduous service, and to keep, withal, an unsoured heart, a bright face, and an open palm. I call you to the higher manhood of all the heroes of the past who have given us this splendid heritage of liberty and religion, of home and literature; to the glorious fellowship of all who by the toil of their hands, by the sweat of their brows, and the blood of their hearts, have made it possible for us to be here, and to be what we are.

Hear the voice that speaks to you, and when Jesus asks, amid all the apostasies and declensions of this modern time, " Will ye also go away?" fear not to answer with Peter, " Lord, to whom shall we go? Thou hast the words of eternal life; and we believe and are sure that thou art the Christ, the Son of the living God."

THE SPIRITUAL PROPHECIES OF CHRISTIAN MANLINESS.

Beloved, now are we the sons of God, and it doth not yet appear what we shall be: but we know that, when he shall appear, we shall be like him; for we shall see him as he is.—1 John iii, 2.

THE Bible, as the vehicle of a supernatural revelation, discloses and sets in a clear light the peculiar glory and greatness of man. This it does in its own *peculiar* way. If it represents him as a wrong-doer, it does not put that wrong-doing on a small, paltry, puny scale; he is a great wrong-doer, and the very essence of his sin is made to consist in an act of audacious rebellion against the Supreme Majesty of the Universe. Only a great being would venture on such an act. If it describes him as in peril on account of his sin, it unfolds that peril as being vast, tremendous, and immeasurable, a peril such as a great transgressor only, not some petty criminal, would be likely to incur. If it describes him as in ruins, it is the ruin of a mighty and glorious being, such as is described in Bushnell's sermon on "The Dignity of Human Nature as Shown by Its Ruins." If he is overtaken by guilt, the matter is of such importance that God himself sets out on a search for him, to rescue him and restore him to righteousness. If he is to be redeemed, it is not by silver or gold, or by the blood of any dumb animal, or by any cold process of merely naturalistic development, but by the incarnation of Divinity, the voluntary condescension of the Great Being to the pain, the suffering, the limitations, and the whole round of experience of our human life. The constant, pervading, and every-where-present assumption is that man is a spiritual being, sprung from God, open to God, made for the highest righteousness, carrying about in him now God-like faculties, equal to direct and intimate communion with the great Original of his being, permeable and inspirable by God. This is the peculiar way in which the Bible makes man great—by relating him to God; and no moral being is great except as he is related to God.

Man's present relation to God, not only, but the vast possibilities of growth that inhere in this truth of his Divine kinship make him great. This is the latent thought of the text. Man *now* is the Son of God, incalculable in the worth and dignity of his being, and his actual greatness, his existing powers point to a future development and glory, a coming investiture of purity and power, that run far beyond the reach of all his present powers of conception. "Beloved, *now* (here, living in the flesh), NOW are we the sons of God"—we have reached that condition already; we are that far along in the line of spiritual development; "but it doth not yet appear what we shall be;" there is not sufficient data to enable us to cipher that out, and so (for to the writers of the New Testament there was no more perfect manhood or being than Jesus Christ) it is declared that we shall be like him when he shall appear.

For several weeks in this place on Sunday evenings we have been studying the nature and power of Christian manliness. In the first lecture its constituent elements were described—what it was not, and what it was—and it was shown that neither genius nor talent nor scholarship nor manners nor knowledge, nor any physical fortitude alone, nor agility nor grace nor beauty, contained the desirable and necessary elements; that three words, more nearly than any others, denoted what it contained—Courage, Dutifulness, Love; that the inspiring soul of genuine manliness was reality; that man should be *true* to the last fiber of his nature, straight in all moral purpose; and that in these and like elements manliness consisted. It was found that it did not depend upon the place of a man's birth, upon his early surroundings, upon the society he mingled with in boyhood or moved in now, whether he had or had not obtained high public position, but that wherever there was a human spirit that so received the right as to bow down to it and serve it, *there* was a man; and that all other kinds of men were simply animals on their road to manhood. In the second lecture the power of manliness was shown in poverty; how it was confronted with the peculiar temptations of that state, and how again and again and again it had triumphed over these seemingly insurmountable obstacles. Such illustrations were given as are afforded by the careers of Horace Greeley and Alexander H. Stephens in this country, and from the great host of men—as good and as true—without their high mental endowments, and who have never come to fame, or to power, or public position. In the third lecture the power of manliness was exhibited in public or civic life, and incidents in the lives of such men as John Stuart Mill, Charles Sumner, Burke, Macaulay, Lincoln, and Garfield were cited to show that men might be brought conspicuously before the public, placed in critical and emergent positions and relations, and not deviate the millionth part of a hair's breadth from righteousness. In the fourth lecture the presence of manliness was shown in the realm of literature, and the careers of Prescott, Wordsworth, Scott, and Shakespeare were briefly recounted in order to show that moral sanity was the substruction of lasting genius, that all genius that did not have underlying it the ethical—the manliness—element was on its way to dissolution and death. In the fifth lecture it was disclosed that in history manliness was sovereign; that the final arbitraments of fame are made to depend upon righteousness, and that all corrupt, false, unrighteous men hasten to such an eclipse of reputation as can only befall those whose great powers have been basely prostituted to unholy purposes. On last Sunday evening it was described as undergoing pain, suffering, obloquy, persecution, defeat, failure; and the careers of Washington, and Milton, and Wellington, and other great men were so far opened up as to show that a man could fight against both wind and tide if the root of the matter was in him.

Now, what is the result or meaning of it all? I am sure, in the first place, that those of you who have been here during the delivery of this course of lectures must have formed a higher estimate of human nature, of the moral greatness of man. It is well that you have; for there are so many unmanly men, so many tricky men, so many disingenuous men, so many cowards and impostors, liars and sneaks in the world, so many cruel men, so many treacherous men, that one must feel refreshed and quickened to be brought into the presence of men who scorn to do a mean thing. Well, now, that is the way we ought to judge human nature. Some people judge human nature as a man would who, going in the fall to an apple-tree hanging full of apples, makes diligent search for all the mean, scrawny, corrupted, tasteless apples there are, and then says: "Ah! these are the kind of apples that this wonderful tree produces!" That is not a fair test for any tree; take the finest apples it will produce under the best conditions, and they are the apples which it ought to produce. That is the kind of apples the tree was intended to produce, and it will produce that kind in genial soil and under proper cultivation. When I see a bungler taking his seat on the organ stool I never blame the organ; I wait for somebody who knows how to evoke its subtle and wonderful harmonies before I pass final judgment on the instrument. And when I want to know how I am to judge men, I will not run around and pick out all the low, base, mean, cowardly men I can find, and say, "This is human nature!" There are some men who would rather be vultures than eagles; there are some people who enjoy a feast of carrion seven days in the week better than any thing else! An eagle never eats carrion; he flies too high to smell it. To judge human nature fairly and honorably, take the best men the race has produced under the most favorable conditions, and remember that every man has in him the same moral capacities. That man yonder may be coarse, he may be vulgar, he may be dishonest, he may be treacherous, he may be warped by his inheritance, his training, his circumstances, but (God pity him!) he has in him all the moral capacities, potentialities, that other men have, and I will not despise him, I will not revile him, I will not judge him narrowly and harshly, for he is my brother, since he is my Father's child.

These lectures have brought before us a large body of most significant facts—facts that need to be accounted for, explained, in some way. They are facts after their own kind, they are ethical facts, spiritual facts, invisible facts, impalpable facts, but *facts* nevertheless. Some people have no idea of a fact except it be as a stone, or a mountain, or a brick wall, or some solid material substance they can put their hands or feet upon. There are those who think that, when you use the word "fact," you must confine it to realities of weight, to facts of number, to facts of color, to purely material facts; but there are facts that you cannot color, or number, or weigh, or touch, or handle, or see, or taste. You buy a pound of coffee from a man, and his scales are half an ounce too light; you have in your hand a pound of coffee less half an ounce—that is one fact; you have in your head the knowledge that your grocer is dishonest—and that is as much a fact as the other is, only you cannot take it up in your hand, weigh it, or carry it off with you in a bundle. Courage is a fact—as much a fact as the Rocky Mountains; it is as much a fact as the granite bases of Mount Washington. Truth—that is as much a fact as the eternal hills. Dutifulness—that is a fact, just as much as a stone, or a picture, or a church, or a cathedral is a fact. Love, brotherliness, kindliness of disposition—these are facts, only they are not palpable, tangible, material, objective facts; they are immaterial, invisible, spiritual.

How shall we account for these facts? Do they suggest any thing? What is their spiritual significance? I propose, first of all, to take that theory of our life proposed by modern unbelief, and apply it to these facts, and see if that will account for them. Modern unbelief may be comprehensively described under four heads: Materialism, Agnosticism, Fate, Annihilation.

Materialism asserts that man is not a double being, but simply an organism of matter; that what we call thought, emotion, will, conscience—all the spiritual elements that are supposed to belong to our natures—are simply the results of certain molecular changes of the cerebral matter. I might even go farther and run the risk of securing a reputation for pedantry by saying that materialism asserts that thought is a secretion of the white and gray matter of the brain under certain molecular conditions. I suppose you understand that; I hope you do; I do not! The theory of materialism is that there is nothing spiritual in man; that all there is of him is the body of matter; highly organized, it is true, but, after all, man is simply a physical being. When you take this small, dwarfish, petty theory of materialism, and put it along-side of the great moral and spiritual facts which we have been studying, you cannot account for them. If we are going to be materialists we ought to be willing to be materialists; we ought fully to accept the logical results of our philosophy. Bacon has taught us, and modern science, following in his wake, has taught us, that we are to accept that theory or hypothesis of any class of facts which most easily and rationally accounts for the greatest number; that hypothesis is to be accepted by means of which the greatest number of facts sort themselves into harmony. You take materialism, and put it along-side of these facts, and none of them sort themselves into harmony.

Agnosticism is an armed neutrality of the intellect as to the existence of God, and especially as to his person, attitude, and character; it neither denies nor affirms that there is a God. There is a milder form of agnosticism with which men of warm, fervid temperaments are tinctured; men who do not deny the existence of a Supreme Something, men who have gone beyond that phase of agnosticism, but who do deny that we know any thing about his character, or that we know, or can know, whether he is a person or not. They assert that he may be a power, or a law, or a stream of tendency, we cannot tell what. Take this theory of agnosticism, and put it along-side of this class of facts, and can you explain them? Can you explain why a weak woman should meekly suffer through long years, on the theory that moral character is indifferent to whoever made the universe and man? I cannot; I stand in the presence of such a woman, suffering, toiling, giving her life for her children in poverty and obscurity, without a murmur or complaint—and then I am told that the Being, or Power, or whoever or whatever it is that created the woman, is utterly indifferent to her, careless whether she suffers or not. Such a theory as that does not account for the facts; it leaves the facts discordant, unrelated, unexplained, inexplicable.

Fate is the doctrine that on the whole we cannot do any better than we have done and are now doing; that our circumstances are such, our environment is such, our inheritances are such, our teachings and teachers have been such, and our work is such that we could not well make any other volitions than those we are now exercising.

I take that theory and put it along-side of the lives of these men who have battled circumstances. I put it along-side of the plain boy in the rude, rough, unpainted New Hampshire farm-house; a boy without learning, without powerful friends. I put it along-side of that poor boy, and I mark his career as he battled circumstances, and beat them down, and trampled on them, and then bravely went on until he came to others and beat them down. And I read in history how men have thus triumphed again and again, and I see in human life all about me men and women who in the presence of difficulties well-nigh insuperable have risen to divine heights and by the power of the spiritual being within them have conquered all difficulties, overcome all obstacles, and I see clearly that this materialistic, mechanical theory of fate and environment will not account for the facts.

The other word descriptive of modern doubt is annihilation; that man, being a material being, having no spirit element in him, is doomed to extinction; that death ends all. Well, my friends, it depends upon whose dead body you are looking at. If you look at that of Guiteau, I do not wonder that you believe in annihilation; but when I look at that of Garfield, I do not believe it. If I was God (I speak with reverence) I would not make such a man as Shakespeare, or Milton, or Lincoln, or Garfield, and then stamp him out forever. What kind of a theory of the universe is that which assigns to things of relatively little value a vast sweep of being, and then to choice, noble, gifted spirits gives only a few troubled years of life? What kind of a theory of the universe is that, I ask, which gives to rocks and hills and oak-trees, to globes and suns, millenniums of life, and to great and noble and princely spirits, like Shakespeare and Milton and Washington and Greeley and Prescott and Wordsworth and Scott, only thirty or forty or fifty years?

> "There is no death! The stars go down
> To rise upon some fairer shore,
> And bright in heaven's jeweled crown
> They shine forever more."

Now, take the Christian hypothesis; take the great first truths of religion and apply them to this body of facts, and let us see if the facts will not at once begin to arrange themselves into order and harmony and consistency. It is a truth of religion that man is a spiritual being, that his body is a temporary dwelling-place of his spirit—as a shell very good to preserve the kernel, as a casket only valuable for the sake of the jewel within—but that the real man is the inside, invisible spirit-man. I take this doctrine that man is a spirit, and I put it along-side the spiritual facts which we have been studying, and I see at once that a spiritual being would be likely to do just such things. Just as I fail to see how a material being could do such things, so do I see why a spiritual being could and would do them; and, therefore, according to the very first postulate of modern science, I accept the latter theory. The former theories fail to account for the facts, the latter theory does account for them.

It is the teaching of religion not only that God *is*, but that he is a Moral Ruler; that he has a distinct, positive, ascertainable, realizable, ethical character; that he seeks righteousness, that he seeks it in his children, that he loves it wherever he sees it; that all the processes of spiritual development that are going on every-where are intended to culminate in such holiness as will enable obedient moral natures to be eternally joined to his nature. I take this doctrine of the ethical character and personality of God, and I take the other truth, that man is God's child, and then I look at these great things that men have done, these great moral acts of which they are the subjects, and they seem to me to be explained under the moral rule of such a God.

It is the teaching of religion that man is morally responsible. It graduates this doctrine of responsibility in proportion to our knowledge, to our opportunities, to our powers, to our light; it demands much where much has been given, and little where little has been given; it beats the man who knew the Lord's will and would not do it with many stripes, and the man who knew little about it with few stripes. Nevertheless it reins men up to a sharp responsibility, declaring, despite all the talk of modern unbelief, that men *are* responsible for what they do, for what they think, for what they become, for what they love and hate; and when I remember these things, and see how these men did act—as though they really were responsible—when I read their careers as they were carrying the nations through dark places, when I read how Lincoln cried out to God in the midst of the great Civil War, striving to rescue this nation from disunion and dismemberment, when I remember these things, I accept the truth of a stringent responsibility for all we do in this world.

Another great truth of religion is immortality. Death, the last mystery and the last enemy, is vincible by Christian manliness. This manliness, which has won such glorious victories in the history of the race, shall not in its turn be conquered by death. It has conquered every thing else, and death shall not be its conqueror. Its eternal home is not in the darksome grave, but among the splendid stars. Death cannot destroy manhood. Did I not say that it was the child of God, and will he, after appointing unto it such splendid victories as it has won here, will he permit the quick grave to swallow it up forever? My friends, the argument for the future life is not physical, not logical, but ethical. Remember the great words of Daniel Webster in his celebrated eulogy on Jeremiah Mason: "Conscience is an inheritance for eternity." What did he mean by it? The facts of conscience are so significant that they transcend time limits. All attempts to bound them by time must fail. "Conscience is an inheritance for ETERNITY." This manhood, though it be indeed developed (as says our great infidel charmer), in "the narrow vale of life," does not see, rising on either side of it, "the cold and barren peaks of two eternities." It sees those peaks, but it sees them clothed with verdure, and radiant in the warm embrace, the glad sunshine of an infinite Father's love. Its vision is beyond those heights. It sees in the eternity that is past the slow unfolding of a mighty plan. It sees in the eternity that is to come the gracious and solemn consummation of that plan. The vast dome of the sky of its hope is lighted up with more than *one* star. Its listening love hears the rustling wings of an uncounted host of angels. Somewhere in the undiscovered country there must be for this regal manhood a perfect temple, an ample home, and an eternal life.

Let us hear, then, the conclusion of the whole matter. Be a mechanic? No! First of all, be a man. Be a merchant? No! You had better, first of all, be a man. Be a lawyer? No! First be a man. Be a banker? No! First be a man. Be a preacher? No! Then be trebly sure that you are a man. Be a man! Be a man!! Be a man!!! Aspire after courage, dutifulness, love. Be true, be open, be genuine, be sincere. Aim at nothing less than the perfect manhood of Jesus Christ. And then, when the end comes, in the fine words of Emerson, "may the heavens open and take you away!"

> "O! who would not a champion be
> In this, the lordlier chivalry?
> Uprouse ye now, brave brother band,
> With honest heart and working hand,

We are but few, toil-tried, but true,
And hearts beat high to dare and do;
O! there be those who ache to see
The day-dawn of our victory!
Eyes full of heart-break with us plead,
And watchers weep, and martyrs bleed;
Work, brothers, work! Work, hand and brain;
We'll win the Golden Age again,
And Love's millennial morn shall rise,
In happy hearts and blessed eyes.
We will, we will, brave champions be,
In this, the lordlier victory!"

THE DESIRE FOR DEATH.

But he himself went a day's journey into the wilderness, and came and sat down under a juniper-tree: and he requested for himself that he might die; and said, It is enough ; now, O Lord, take away my life ; for I am not better than my fathers.—1 Kings xix, 4.

THERE is a striking contrast between divine and human biographies. The Bible gives the whole of a human character. It neither unduly extols the virtues nor extenuates the vices of its martyrs and heroes, saints and apostles. It does not labor to conceal the frailties and sins which every-where attach to our imperfect human nature. It does not seek to cover up and hide the follies and the infirmities, the crimes and treacheries and apostasies, of which not a few of its prominent subjects were guilty. With a certain noble fearlessness, it relates the falls and weaknesses of its prophets, psalmists, lawgivers, kings, judges, priests, and apostles. Human biographies are careful to relate only the meritorious actions of their subjects. One would suppose in reading them that great and good men lived absolutely stainless, faultless lives. No moral overthrows, no glaring faults, no weak and despairing hours, no bitter repentance of excuseless sins are allowed to disfigure the fair record of spotless human lives. The guilt, the weakness, the failures, the contradictions that are nowhere separable from men are diligently excluded from any of the religious biographies and works we so eagerly devour. Modern religious biographies "give us not only the cream of the lives of their heroes, but very often that cream is churned into butter." In the text we have fearlessly and frankly related the sudden terror and flight, and the subsequent discouragement and despondency, of Elijah. In the majority of religious biographies such an incident would never have found a place. It would have been thought fatally discreditable to a modern religious hero to have acted as Elijah is here reported to have acted, and his biographer would certainly have resorted to every known literary device in order to conceal his weakness and disgrace.

This refreshing truthfulness of the Bible constitutes one of the most convincing evidences of its superhuman origin. The Bible is God's book, and God can afford to tell the truth. If uninspired and calculating men had written the Bible, they would have carefully excluded the slightest reference to the intoxication of Noah, the impatience of Moses, the deceit of Abraham, the greed of Jacob, the adultery of David, the intolerance of John, and the denial of Peter. God has given us a book true to our manifold human life. The good and bad, the base and the noble, of our humanity are here. Its high resolves and its poor performance, its lofty yearnings and its mean selfishness, its holy prayers and its impure deeds, its exalted bravery and its miserable cowardice, its glorious angelic affinities and its swinish appetites, all are here. God was not in a hurry to complete his Bible, he waited four thousand years; but when he gave it to the world it was a real, true, brave book. It is a faithful record of human failure and human success. Let us reverently thank God for the Bible as it is, and not as a modern assembly of divines would have made it.

The outlines of a strange and unexpected picture are sketched for us by the text. Not that there is any thing passing strange in a man becoming disgusted with himself, growing weary of human life, and wanting once for all to rid himself of its duties and responsibilities, its sorrows and burdens. Not alone in the wilderness of Southern Judea, in a remote age, among an alien people; but now, to-day, here in America, men are crying, " It is enough. Now, O Lord, take away my life. The sin is enough, the suffering is enough, the ignorance, the struggle, the toil, the pain is enough, the darkness is enough, the failure is enough. Let me die. Release me from the strife and pain and defeat." No! There is nothing remarkably strange in all this. But that Elijah wanted to die, that Elijah grew weary of life, that Elijah should flee from duty, that Elijah should play the coward, that Elijah should distrust God, that he who had defied Ahab face to face, dictating his own terms; that he who had boldly confronted the four hundred and fifty priests of Baal on Mt. Carmel, and put them all to death; that this man, who by a word had called down fire from heaven, should flee at the threat of a heathen woman, and should throw himself under a juniper-tree and ask for death, confessing that he was no better than his fathers, all this is strange and unexpected. Elijah, then, was a man after all. He, too, had his weak, despondent, faithless hours. He, too, grew weary of the toil and strife. Like ourselves, he thought the evil in himself and the world too great to be conquered. "It is enough: now, O Lord, take away my life." We see, then, that Elijah belonged to a humanity like our own. He was not a celestial, but a human, being. I am glad, not that Elijah failed at a critical hour, not that he became disheartened, weary of himself and the world, and wanted to die; but that when he did do so the Bible was brave enough to tell us of it. That one experience unites us all to Elijah. We have our hours of discouragement and flight. We, too, grow faithless. We, too, would fain seek the rest of death. Let us not on this account judge ourselves too swiftly or too harshly. A great prophet, yea, one of the greatest of the prophets, did the like before us; and as there was hope and recovery, and subsequent work for him, so there may be hope and restoration and new life for us. Let us not forget that true Christian progress is made by a divine forgetting of the past.

Why did Elijah want to die? What were the causes of his weakness and hopelessness? There are two probable reasons for his exceptional conduct.

First, it may have been because his sublime victory on Mt. Carmel was not instantly followed by as great results as he ardently desired. Ahab, the Jewish king of Samaria, was married to Jezebel, a heathen princess. This woman had overthrown the religion of the Jews, and had introduced the worship of Baal and Astarte. The whole land was overrun with idolatry. The aim of Elijah was to overthrow Baalism and restore monotheism. His prophetic soul burned with indignation against the impure religion of the Phenicians, and he longed to see the people restored to their ancient spiritual faith in one unseen, almighty, eternal God. On Mt. Carmel, God had answered his simple, earnest prayer, and the people had shouted, "The Lord, he is the God! The Lord, he is the God!" Doubtless, Elijah expected that this was but the beginning of a series of splendid miracles, which should have their final issue in the utter extirpation of the foreign idolatry. But he was disappointed. Things went on in their usual course, and the final victory seemed as far removed as ever. Elijah may have been dissatisfied with God's way of working. He wanted instant and complete triumph. He could brook no delay. His restless and eager soul demanded the precipitate destruction of the religion of Jezebel. His despondency may have been caused by what he deemed the tardiness of God.

Secondly, Elijah may have desired death simply because of shame at his impulsive and ignoble flight from Jezebel. It will be remembered that after

Elijah's triumph over the priests of Baal he took them to the brook Kishon and slew four hundred of them there with his own hands. When Ahab related to Jezebel all that Elijah had done, and withal how he had slain all the prophets with the sword, she determined to wreak swift and summary vengeance upon him. No sooner had Ahab finished his story than she sent a messenger to Elijah, saying, "So let the gods do to me, and more also, if I make not thy life as the life of one of them by to-morrow about this time." It is related that when Elijah "saw that," that is, when he heard of Jezebel's threat, "he went for his life," and came to Beersheba. Strange he never thought that God was stronger than the rage of this idolatrous woman. He doubted God, else her threat would have been powerless. His bitter prayer for death may have been extorted from him at the thought of his distrust of God. "I am no better than my fathers." He had honestly desired, eagerly hoped, to be better, but here he was—just like his fathers; faithless as they had been faithless! Better than his fathers—and lo! he had trembled and fled at the threat of a wicked woman! "It is enough, Lord. I am just like all the rest. Take away my life."

Is it right for good men ever to desire death? If so, when, and in what spirit? If we desire death in the spirit of Paul, it is not culpable or blameworthy. In his letter to the Corinthians Paul says: "We are confident, I say, and willing rather to be absent from the body, and to be present with the

Lord." In his Philippian letter he says that he is "in a strait betwixt two, having a desire to depart, and to be with Christ; which is far better: nevertheless to abide in the flesh is more needful for you." Paul was not a complainer. He was not an idler. He was not a coward. He did not desire to die that he might be released from labor. He was not weary of the battle against the evil that is in the world. He expressly says that his desire to depart and be with Christ is restrained and modified by a knowledge of the fact that he was still needed by the Church on earth. He desired death, not as a cessation of labor, but as an admission into a higher, nobler, worthier ministry. He would die only that he might do more and better work. He desired a departure out of this world that he might have more and fuller life. His hope was that mortality might be swallowed up of life. He would be unclothed, only that he might be clothed upon with the perfect and unshadowed life of love and worship. In this spirit, and with these aims, it is not wrong to desire release from the present life. It is always right to seek freedom when emancipation means enfranchisement.

I. We are not to desire death because God does not work exactly after our fashion, as, perhaps, not as quickly as we desire him to work. The intense, earnest workers of this world are very prone to become impatient with God, as well as with their tardy fellow-workmen. They have such a sharp sense of the evil that is here, such a tender sympathy with suffering, such a burning hatred of sin, such a keen desire for the recovery of men to holiness and love, such a passionate yearning for the social and moral regeneration of society, that they can scarcely abide God's patient methods. So it was with Elijah. He would have God rend the heavens, and descend with an army of angels, utterly to consume the idolatry that had bewitched and lured away the Jewish people. He was not willing to allow space for the working of natural processes to wean the people from their accursed idolatry. Nor are we willing that by natural spiritual processes men shall learn the beauty of holiness and the deformity of sin. We are for precipitating things. We are for demanding the employment of supernatural power where natural power, where natural agencies only, can finally and effectually avail. God works slowly, but he does his work well. When once he has completed a task it is done forever. We are impatient because we have but a morsel of time in which to work. Not so with him. He is the Father of the everlasting ages. A thousand years in his sight are but as yesterday when it is past, and as a watch in the night. His mills grind exceeding slow, but they grind; and they grind exceeding fine. We are to do that part of the work which God has allotted to us humbly, lovingly, thoroughly, and then, with a serene and unquestioning faith, we are to leave the results with him. You and your work and this world are safe with God.

II. We are not to desire death because we have

failed in some trial-hour, because we have ignobly fled when we should have bravely stood, because our high, fine, noble ideals lie withered and dying at our feet. His contact with Jezebel was the trial-hour of Elijah's life. In that hour, of all hours, he should have stood firm and steadfast. But he yielded and fled. There come like trial-hours to all of us. We may not be aware of their approach, and we may not fully comprehend all that is wrapped up in them. They may even seem insignificant to us. They are, nevertheless, the real trial-hours of our lives. They test us. They try what sort of stuff we are made of. They touch the core of our manhood. How many of us go down in these hours! How many of us are unable to stand the testing process! The bait of evil is too glittering and seductive for all the manhood we have, and we bite—to find but an empty hook.

With what high, pure, lofty ideals did we all begin life! Like Elijah, we were determined to be better than our fathers. Where now are our high purposes, our chivalric aims, our holy resolves? We have dragged them down, and they are covered with the common dust of life. It is when men become sadly conscious of these things that they run away from the unfulfilled tasks of life, and, discouraged and despondent, ask God for death. But these are not the hours in which we should desire to die. It is not when he has proven recreant to his high duty that the soldier is to ask for his discharge from the army. Rather he should then, with tears, if need be, beseech his commander to send him back to the most difficult and dangerous post, that by his future courageous fidelity he may shame and retrieve the cowardice of the past. Not in hours that follow failure and recreancy and sin are we to desire death. Then most fervently should we beseech God for a new lease of life and a fresh trial, that we may atone for the guilty and bitter past by the more noble and valorous action of the future.

III. We are not to desire death because we think we have suffered enough. What an army of sufferers God has in this world! If they were to march past us this morning, what an array of anguish they would present. Think of the blind, of the deaf, of the dumb, of the deformed, of the crippled, of the weak, of the hopeless invalids! How many are suffering from physical causes! How many who are never free from pain! How many are slowly coughing their lives away! How many wasting with fevers! How many are outcasts from society through no fault of their own! How many who are suffering the stings of grinding poverty! How many are torn and rent with hideous doubts! How many parents' hearts are gashed with sorrow at the moral recreancy of their children! How many men are broken down at the very threshold of life, its golden prizes seemingly just within their grasp! How many weary hearts are saying to-day, "It is enough; now, O Lord, take away my life!" How many white-faced sufferers are looking up to heaven, praying God to release them! How many sightless eye-balls are longing for that land where the Lord God shall give them light! How many fiercely tempted, fiend-goaded souls are seeking with unutterable longing a city far, far above the assoilments of sin. Ye penitent, suffering, struggling souls, judge not too swiftly your wise and compassionate Father. Not the marble, but the sculptor, is to judge of the finished work. " Whom the Lord loveth he chasteneth." God will soon deal the last stroke, the work will be done, and the beauty of the Lord your God shall be upon you forever!

It was well for Elijah that God did not answer his impulsive and passionate prayer. The time and manner of his death were better in the divine hands than in his own gloomy and despondent thoughts. God had large and noble work for him to do, and right well did he do it. The lonely and discouraged prophet was guided to the solemn and majestic Horeb, and there, amid its awful solitudes, he learned that there were seven thousand that had not bowed the knee, and that God was in the still small voice, as well as in the thunder and tempest and earthquake and whirlwind and fire. And then, when his work was done at last, the chariot of fire and horses of fire came to take him; "and Elijah went up by a whirlwind into heaven."

Let us not seek to appoint the hour when we would cease our terrestrial life and work. Let God choose the time and surroundings for our departure. We may have despondent hours, gloomy hours, faithless hours. Let us not hastily and impetuously desire death in them. God reserves better, braver, worthier hours for us. In them let us die—or, rather, in them let us be crowned: for that which we call death is but a translation from darkness to light, from unsatisfied yearning to perpetual fruition, from time and toil and men to eternal life in God!

THE IDENTIFICATION OF DIVINITY WITH HUMANITY.

For which cause he is not ashamed to call them brethren.—Heb. ii, 11.

THERE need be no misinterpretation of the teaching of the text and its connections. Jesus Christ, more than man, higher than angel, an altogether extraordinary and unique Being, one who thought it not robbery to be equal with the Highest, voluntarily took upon himself our nature, became in very deed subject to the conditions and limitations under which men live, that he might rescue them from sin and vitally unite them to God. "For both he that sanctifieth and they who are sanctified are all of one," that is, of one nature, experience, order of development—the nature, experience, and order of development of the one being precisely similar to the nature, experience, and order of development of the other. "For which cause," that is, on which account, because of this likeness, this identity, of nature and experience, "he," that is, Jesus, "is not ashamed to call them brethren." Jesus openly and conspicuously recognized his brotherhood with man in distinct, positive, and unmistakable terms. His message to the disciples on the resurrection morning through Mary was, "Go to my brethren, and say unto them, I ascend to my Father and your Father, and to my God and your God." So, also, in that remarkable discourse which is contained in the twenty-fifth chapter of Matthew: "Inasmuch as ye have done it unto one of the least of these my brethren, ye have done it unto me." We see thus how completely, and at every point, Jesus joined himself to human nature. The text raises for our consideration the high and grateful theme of the identification of Divinity with humanity.

He who is here spoken of as the Sanctifier, and as of one nature with the sanctified, is described in terms that endow him with the sole and peculiar attributes of Divinity. In the opening of this epistle we are told that God, who had heretofore spoken to men by the prophets, has in these last days spoken unto us by his Son. This Son is declared to be appointed Heir of all things, and to be the Person through whom the worlds were made. He is said to uphold all things by the word of his power, and to be the brightness of the Father's glory and the express image of his person. He is compared with men, and is set far above them. He is compared with angels, and is lifted transcendently above them in nature, dignity, authority, and power; yea, the angels of God are commanded to worship him. Thus we see Jesus exalted in every conceivable way by every form of language, by the possession of the most supernal and divine attributes, until, as he is raised from height to height, touching at last the very summit of the uncreated life, we are constrained to cry out with Thomas, "My Lord and my God." Then it is, when he is raised to the highest point of his exaltation, when he is carried up to the very apex of being, then it is that he is described as entering upon his mighty humiliation: then it is that he is pictured as assuming our nature and entering upon the actual experience of human life, work, temptation, suffering, and death. "We see Jesus, who was made for a little while inferior to the angels, for the suffering of death, crowned with glory and honor; that he by the grace of God should taste death for every man." He is said to have come to the moral leadership of the race, in other words, to have been "perfected," through sufferings, and through such sufferings as are common to men. As the children were "partakers of flesh and blood, he also himself likewise took part of the same." He became obedient unto death, "that through death he might destroy him that had the power of death, that is, the devil; and deliver them who through fear of death were all their lifetime subject to bondage." He rejected the nature and estate of angels, and took upon him the seed of Abraham. In order that he might be a merciful and faithful High-priest, he was in ALL THINGS made like unto his brethren. We see in the clear, revealing, concentered light of this teaching how real, how complete and thorough-going was the union of Divinity and humanity in the person of Jesus Christ. "For both he that sanctifieth and they who are sanctified are all of one: for which cause he is not ashamed to call them brethren."

The grateful perfume of heaven is on this passage. It is richly odorous of the skies. Like the fresh, dewy tuberose by the bedside of the wan invalid, it suggests the whole garden of flowers from which it came. It is as a branch of the great tree of life, hanging so low as to be within reach of men's hands, that they may pluck and eat and live!

If, now, the question be asked, Why this amazing condescension of Divinity, and its intimate union with humanity? the final and sufficient answer is to be found in God's mighty love and tender compassion for man. This sacrificial condescension and humiliation was born, not of wrath or hatred, nor of any supposed governmental necessity, but of the free, the boundless grace and kindness of God our Father. Why does a mother enter into real, not simulated, sympathy with her little child, bearing its sorrows, carrying its infirmities, sharing its joys? Because of the mother-love that is in her. So God, impelled by his love, becomes one with man, sharing our human estate and condition in all things save sin.

1. The truth of this passage reveals the precise point at which, and with how great fullness, Christianity meets and answers the deepest and strongest yearnings, the unappeasable hunger, of the human heart. "Where is God, that we may find him?" This is the universal question of time. It is as an-

cient as Job. "O that I knew where I might find him; that I might come even to his seat: I would order my cause before him, and fill my mouth with arguments." The thinker, perplexed with life's enigmas, has asked, Where is He? Likewise the doer, the sufferer, the slave, the guilty penitent, the oppressed, the lonely and sorrow-burdened, all alike have asked, Where is He?

Man has ever been pursued by the thought that God, alike by the quality and the volume of his nature, is widely, possibly impassably, separated from us. Hence the feeling that only by the interposition of an anointed priest, or of an infallible Church, or of a bleeding sacrifice, or by gloomy austerities, can man traverse the wide and desolate wastes, and draw near to God. This, in epitome, is the history of man's efforts to effect a union of Divinity and humanity; namely, an age-long struggle to carry our frail, imperfect, temptable humanity up to Divinity.

Observe how Christianity meets this want, feeds this hunger, of our hearts. God is already nigh us, if we would but receive him. He is not far from any one of us, if haply we would seek for him. Divinity is close to humanity. There is a reunion of Divinity and humanity, not by the slow, labored, difficult, perilous ascent of humanity to Divinity, but by the descent of Divinity to humanity. In a word, we do not seek him so much as he seeks us. We do not find him so much as he finds us. We need not ascend on high to bring Christ down, nor descend into the depths to bring him up; for he is already in our hearts. He has come to us, entered into our estate, partaken of our nature, been subject to our experiences, and is not ashamed to call us brethren. We need no surpliced priest, no ancient rite, no bleeding lamb, no charm of words, to come into union with him; we need only, with truly penitent hearts, to turn away from our sins, to accept his love, and to be obedient to his words.

Does not Christianity thus really and graciously discover, and amply, yea, gloriously, satisfy the deepest yearnings, the holiest longings, the divinest hunger of our hearts?

2. This doctrine of the identification of the Divine nature with man's nature gives intelligent emphasis to the real purpose and the true mission of the Church in the world. What is the Church? What does it exist for? A society of men and women who acknowledge with their lips, and who seek to realize in their spiritual life, the union of Divinity and humanity. The Church has for its highest, its special and distinctive, object the revelation to the world of this experimental knowledge of God! It is not of the nature of a co-operative insurance society. It is not a social club. It is not a Sunday lectureship on ethics, or the philosophy of religion. It is not a jealously guarded hospital, into which no patient can be admitted without correctly answering a long list of hypothetical or merely technical questions. The Church is a society of men and women confessing the union of God with man, recognizing

Identification of Divinity with Humanity. 131

the actual brotherhood of Jesus with all men, and hence the brotherhood of all men with each other; and it seeks to make this union and this brotherhood real and vital, actual and potent.

How, then, may we ascertain the existence of a genuine Christian Church in the community? Not by any external or ceremonial or intellectual sign or symbol, but by the discovery of a society of people who know God and have received his life. How would you prove to a man shivering with the cold on a bleak December day that there is fire in your stove? The quickest and surest way would be to bring him near enough to your stove to feel the heat. Heat is the best possible proof of fire, and there is no surer or more convincing evidence of the reality and nearness of heat than to feel the warmth.

3. As, in the far and wide-revealing light of this Divine teaching, we see the folly, the ingratitude, and the loss of those who separate themselves from God, so, on the other hand, do we see the liberation and enfranchisement, the honor and glory of the soul that seeks the union of its life with God. What is a sinner? Passing by the ordinary definitions, let us try to answer in the light of the text. He is one who has separated himself from God; he is one who refuses the present union of his nature with divinity. What folly, misery, ingratitude, loss! What shall we say of the branch which, restive and impatient, severs itself from the vine? What would we think of this earth of ours growing im-

patient of its dependence on gravity, unfastening itself from law and order, swinging out of its orbit, casting off its allegiance to the sun? The degradation of the prodigal feeding the swine consists in this: that he was made for better things, and threw them away himself. Our subject teaches us that man was made for blessed union with God, and when he separates, divorces, cuts himself off from divinity, we see in a new light the folly, the guilt, the misery, and the degradation of the sinful life.

Men sometimes resent appeals to enter upon the life of obedience to God, as though the act involved something humiliating, unmanly, weak, and dishonorable. The glory of the self-willed, wandering, outcast child is its return to its old home and its old obedience. The prodigal honors and enfranchises himself when he sets his conscience toward duty, his heart toward his father, his face toward home. See the wandering globe, tired of its willful, zigzag, eccentric course, returning to its orbit of harmony and order. As men dishonor themselves when they cut loose from God, so they honor themselves when they return to him. He is our home. He is the source of our life, light, righteousness, and love. See yonder Prince, anciently and honorably descended, heir to a throne and a kingdom, clothed in filthy, tattered raiment, despising his birthright, madly refusing the royal purple offered him, stamping it in the filth with angry feet! Is he dishonored when he throws away his rags, accepts the purple, and starts for his throne and scepter?

"For which cause he is not ashamed to call them brethren." He who once had not where to lay his head is now set down at the right hand of God, clothed with power and authority and majesty ineffable! He who once was despised and rejected of men, a man of sorrows, and acquainted with grief, is now raised far above all principality, and power, and might, and dominion, and every name that is named, not only in this world, but also in that which is to come, and on his brow, thorn-pierced no more, is set the lustrous diadem of the universe. He has been glorified with the glory that he had with the Father before the worlds were. I know not the measure, the quality, the fullness, the manifoldness of that glory. I may not count the number of those who stand in his presence, forever released from evil, and ignorance, and imperfection, and struggle, and pain, and loss, and death. To me it is not given to know the rapture of their devotion, the fervor of their worship, the purity of their love, the sweep of their song, the high nobility of their tireless work. There before Him, order after order, rank on rank, hierarchy above hierarchy, they flame, and worship, and adore, and serve—angels and archangels, cherubim and seraphim, principalities and powers, thrones and dominions. I know not the breadth, or length, or wealth, or splendor, or power, or security of that city of which he is the king—its streets of pure gold, its walls of jasper, its gates of pearl, into which pour the honor and glory of the nations; a city which has no need of the sun or the moon to shine in it, for the glory of God does lighten it, and the Lamb is the Light thereof. The full, unshaded blaze of his resplendent, eternal glory would blind our poor, weak eyes, but, though I cannot now see the King in his beauty, in the land that is far off, this I know: that as he beholds this rolling globe, speeding through the vast and silent spaces, carrying its burden of guilt and mystery and tears, with its myriads of sinning, suffering, struggling, yearning men, HE is not ashamed, even in that high presence, and amid the radiance of that ample and unwasting splendor, to turn his eyes hitherward, and say, "*Yonder*, YONDER, are my brethren!" He is not ashamed of his brotherhood with us. Shall we, how dare we, be ashamed of our brotherhood with Him? Confess it, yield to it, live in it, rejoice in it, work and suffer and die in it, be ennobled and purified and exalted by it this day, and forever.

MODERN PROGRESS AN ENCOURAGEMENT TO MISSIONARY ZEAL.

According to this time it shall be said of Jacob and of Israel, What hath God wrought!—Num. xxiii, 23.

I WISH to speak to you, from these words, on modern progress as an incentive to missionary zeal.

The definite, comprehensive aim of the modern missionary enterprise is the complete, universal triumph of Christianity. It will be the moral subjugation of the entire race. It is nothing short of the recovery to spiritual manhood, after the lofty and perfect model furnished by Jesus Christ, of all dwellers upon this globe. This great end will not be reached when all heathen countries shall have outwardly and nominally received Christianity as England or the United States have received it. When all moral beings that live on this globe shall have voluntarily and joyously accepted Jesus Christ as a Divine Saviour, and shall have entirely submitted themselves to his rule of life, the triumph of the missionary enterprise is assured.

There is nowhere furnished us a surer test of Christian faith, devotion, and enthusiasm than just here. It is precisely at this point that we find even in Christian hearts the most secret and dangerous obstacle to the cause of Christian missions. The enterprise seems so vast, inclusive, and far-reaching, involving, as it does, governments, nations, and centuries; the work seems so intricate, so complex, so difficult, so slow, so stupendous, that, in spite of ourselves, certain undefined, secret, benumbing doubts are engendered, even in loyal, earnest Christian hearts. It is to be feared that, with any thing like an intelligent knowledge of what is really contemplated by the great missionary enterprise, few of us have ever found our faith equal to a clear, steady, and ardent acceptance of the sublime triumph. It is my purpose to take a recent period of human history, and show, by its wonderful progress in all the various elements of a sound, enduring civilization, that the end at which we aim is actually possible of accomplishment; yea, that these conspicuous developments of history clearly, irresistibly demonstrate that we are the subjects of a large and beneficent law of progress; that the obvious, actual, undisputed facts of the history of the last four hundred years do furnish Christian faith the greatest possible encouragement to believe in the ultimate triumph of the missionary cause.

First, as to the facts. The actual condition of the so-called Christian world toward the close of the fifteenth century, or four hundred years ago, say 1486, or just six years before Columbus discovered America, is scarcely realizable by men of the present time. The physical, social, political, intellectual, and moral condition of the continent of Europe at that time was indeed wretched and deplorable. The population of the entire continent had scarcely doubled

Encouragement to Missionary Zeal. 137

in one thousand years, and the death-rate was one in twenty-five. Physicians and their remedies were derided and depressed, and the vain and fantastic virtues of shrine-cure were extravagantly extolled. The great cities were without sewers, without lamps at night, without any efficient or rational sanitary or police regulations. The war-like nobles and the powerful prelates lived in idleness, splendor, voluptuousness, and luxury. The people were every-where sunk in sloth, ignorance, filth, poverty, and crime. In Paris and London the houses were of wood daubed with clay, and thatched with straw and reeds. Carpets were an unknown luxury. No attempts were made at drainage, but the putrefying garbage and rubbish were simply thrown out of the door or window, very often to the great discomfort of the luckless passer-by. In 1430, Pope Pius II. visited the British Isles, and the journal he kept on his travels is preserved to this day in the library of the Vatican. He describes the houses of the peasantry as constructed of stones put together without mortar, the roofs were of turf, and a stiffened bull's hide served for a door. The food consisted of coarse vegetable products, such as raw peas, and often the bark of trees. In some places they were unacquainted with bread. A man was considered to be in circumstances of great ease if he could afford to have fresh meat once a week for his dinner. The social bonds were every-where relaxed, and a gross and terrible licentiousness prevailed in all ranks of society. Science was necromancy, chemistry was alchemy, astronomy was astrology, philosophy was a fatuous search after the stone that would turn everything into gold, and religion had largely become a most wretched and execrable superstition. Genuine scientific study was almost unknown, while the few votaries of science to be found were denounced as heretics, apostates, or infidels. Intellectual torpor and stagnation every-where existed, except in the immediate vicinity of the monasteries and universities. The art of printing was comparatively crude and imperfect. There were no railways, no telegraphs, no steam-printing presses, no newspapers, no cheap books, NO SCHOOLS FOR THE PEOPLE. The bodies and labor and time of men belonged to the king, while their intellects and consciences were owned by the pope and his ministers. Kings reigned by divine right, and the pope was the vice-gerent of Almighty God. To question the sovereignty of either in their respective realms was swift and certain death. The shameless practice of selling indulgences was confessed to be the most lucrative source of revenue to the see of St. Peter. Tyranny and superstition in the sacred name of religion had combined their energies to rob and oppress the people, and the day of their enlightenment, liberty, and enfranchisement seemed indefinitely postponed.

Let us seek to give our brief summary of historical facts artistic grouping, to the end that they may make a more striking and vivid impression on the mind, and that they may be the longer remembered. It is one of those lovely evenings which Italy alone furnishes; for, no sun is brighter, no skies are bluer, no airs are softer than those of Italy—the land of classic memories, the land of eloquence, music, poetry, and song. The windows of the Vatican are open to catch any freshening breeze that may blow from the Mediterranean. Gathered in a magnificent drawing-room are his holiness, the blessed Innocent VIII., and his cardinals, with a royal visitor or two, perhaps Henry VII. of England. Suddenly, without a word of warning, without a single premonition, as Nathan unbidden appeared before David, as the lone and terrible Elijah rose up in the way before Ahab in his golden chariot, a bold prophet in strange, startling attire, his eyes glowing with the light divine, stands in their presence to announce the course of events in the next four centuries. Startled, bewildered, paralyzed with a strange fear, they listen in silence. Nothing could have seemed more unreal than the burden of his prophecy. He prophesied that before the close of the nineteenth century, or within the four hundred years, the pope should lose more than one third of his spiritual children; that all truly intelligent men would regard with ill-concealed scorn the spurious miracles of the Dark Ages; that an Augustinian monk of Germany, then a babe of three years, would forever sunder the Church in twain; that the pope should be entirely divested of his temporal power and be restricted to the exercise of his purely spiritual functions; that the spherical form of the earth and its daily revolution round the sun would be convincingly demonstrated; that the poor man would travel faster in his day than noblemen could five hundred years ago; that the light in the poor man's house would be superior to that of the king's palace; that for a trifling sum he would have better pictures of his wife and child than kings then possessed; that the right of the many to tax the entire community in order that the blessing of public education might every-where open the doors of opportunity and hope to struggling, aspiring men would be generally acknowledged; that men should travel on land with ease, rapidity, and safety at the rate of forty miles per hour; that iron vessels, propelled by steam, should cross vast oceans in a week; that daily newspapers should be circulated by the million, containing news from all quarters of the globe received during the previous twenty-four hours by electric telegraph; that a plain, humble, prayerful, studious man was even then alive, and begging his way from one European court to another, who, after incredible toils and perils, should discover the western world; that there should be developed in this newly discovered world a mighty republic, surpassing, in its marvelous growth, expansion, and prosperity, all the golden dreams of sages, poets, and reformers: that this republic should be forever free from all ecclesiastical control and dictation; that in 1880 its population should be over fifty millions, but five millions of whom should in any way acknowledge the absurd pretensions of the pope; that the birth of this republic should be brought about by the revolt of English colonists against the cruel and shortsighted tyranny of George III., a king of England, and that, by the dawn of the twentieth century of this era, progress in science, democracy in government, liberty in politics, toleration in religion, and unfettered investigation of the truth should be axiomatic truths among all truly civilized men! What a prophet! And what a prophecy! How the prophecy would be scorned and derided! And what short work they would have made of such a prophet! How unnatural, yea, how almost impossible, would many of these things have seemed to these men! We live to know that these prophecies have been amply and gloriously fulfilled; that in casting the horoscope of the future our prophet did not utter a single idle word or indulge in one extravagant promise.

Let us take a little closer and more searching glance at the astonishing, the almost incredible, intellectual and moral progress of this period. Let us see—we are back to 1486. One great intellectual and moral idea underlies the vast, the amazing improvement or growth of modern times. That idea, expressed in its simplest form, is, *that every man belongs to himself; that every man has the right to develop himself, body, intellect, conscience, according to his best knowledge.* Martin Luther builded better than he knew. He was contending not merely against the shameless sale of indulgences by Tetzel, but he was doing brave battle for the sacredness and inviolability of the individual conscience. Leo X. stood for spiritual tyranny; for the right of Rome to control the minds and consciences of men. Martin Luther stood for spiritual liberty; for the right of men to culture their own minds and worship God as their own consciences dictated. It was this divine truth that gave power and victory to the Reformation, and from thence directed the whole course and current of modern history. It passed, first, into the sphere of speculative political philosophy, and, thence working its way into the realm of practical politics, it revolutionized governments. It stirred the peasants to rise against the barons of Germany. It fomented the parliamentary conflicts of England. It solemnly arraigned a king at the bar of public justice as a criminal against the people. It pronounced and executed the sentence of death against Charles I.; drove the bigoted and tyrannical James II. from his throne and his kingdom; curtailed the prerogatives of the sovereign; enlarged the liberties of the people, and created all those just and beneficent reforms which to-day constitute the strength and pride and glory of the British empire. It inaugurated the French Revolution—that immense and awful act of justice; overthrew the ancient aristocratic *régime*; opened the eyes of the people to their just political rights, and made it possible for France, for Europe, yea, for the world some day to be free. It crossed the wide Atlantic with the Pilgrim fathers in the cabin of the *Mayflower*, and found a congenial home amid the wilds of the New World. It strengthened the hearts of our forefathers for the revolutionary struggle. It fired the first shot at Lexington, that "alarm gun of the world." It fought the battles of Concord and Bunker Hill, inspired the Declaration of Independence, and dictated the imperishable sentiment that "all men are born and created free and equal; that they are endowed by their Creator with certain inalienable rights, and that among these are life, liberty, and the pursuit of happiness."

The time and our purpose forbid any tarrying for the consideration of the general lessons here involved, much as we would delight to rest for that purpose. Many important and searching questions are decisively answered by this rapid historical survey, which should bring cheer and hope, stimulation and courage, to every lover of his kind. What, however, is the lesson to the Christian? Is there any thing here to strengthen his faith? Is there any thing here to show that *his* God is in history? Let us rather ask, Is there not here every thing to strengthen his faith? to show that his God is, indeed, the God of history? Do not the actual facts furnish ample ground for the largest and brightest hopes? Do they not furnish sufficient reason for his faith in the final and complete victory of Christian missions? Do not these facts show conclusively that we are under the sway of some vast, noble, divine law of progress? Do they not give the death-blow to pessimism? Do they not show that "God reigns?" What should chill our zeal, or dampen our ardor, or stagger our faith now? Where are the limits of this law? Who shall fix its boundaries? Where now is the impossibility of the spiritual conquest of the world by Jesus Christ? We dare not attempt to limit or to put a boundary to the discoveries, the inventions, the progress, of the future in material things. So, also, in the higher realm of ideas, conduct, thought, morals, religion. Do not these facts clearly show the trend? Who, after this review, will talk of chance or chaos, of there being no purpose or plan in human affairs? The one great lesson of all modern progress is the encouragement thus furnished to the Christian faith that the glorious Gospel of the blessed God is destined to win a universal triumph!

The great missionary enterprise, what is it? The missionary "idea," in itself considered, is simply that of love seeking to bless those who need love; it is love going forth from its pleasant home, lordly mansion, or princely palace to rescue the perishing; it is love seeking to provide homes for the homeless, friends for the friendless, help for the helpless, food for the starving, guides for the lost, mercy for the guilty, holiness for the sinful, hope for the despairing. This idea is not, indeed, peculiar to "modern" times. It is at least as old as Christianity; for Jesus himself was the first great Missionary, leaving the glory he had with his Father before the worlds were, and coming here to seek and save the lost. Yea, it is older still. It is as old as the gracious and kindly thoughts of God toward weak and sinful men, for, in the infinite heart of God, Jesus was a Lamb slain from the foundation of the world! The missionary idea! Tell me when first the heart of God throbbed with love for the sinful and the guilty, the needy, the weak, and the suffering; tell me that, and I will tell you how old the missionary "idea" is! This is the central, vitalizing idea of missions—love seeking the perishing, knowledge using itself for the ignorant, strength serving weakness, comfort relieving distress, God seeking man, not to condemn and smite, but to save and bless, him! This is the great missionary enterprise in its idea, essence, spirit. It contemplates the complete moral conquest, the spiritual recovery, of the human race. This, and nothing short of this, is its glorious and sublime end! This is our work, and a great, glorious, blessed work it is!

Is there no encouragement to our faith in this work in the growth of this four hundred years? Does not "modern progress" include as one of its most significant facts the birth, the growth, and the triumph of Protestant missions? In 1792 the first Protestant missionary society was organized by the Baptists, with a subscription of less than seventy dollars. It was in 1788, at Northampton, that William Carey first attempted to rouse his brethren to their duty to spread the Gospel in foreign parts. In the year 1800, there were eight feeble Protestant missionary societies in the whole world! For many years this idea had to struggle against a mighty tide of ignorance, prejudice, and selfishness in order to find room for itself. How wonderful has been its growth since the beginning of the present century! Why, only last year the Protestants of Great Britain and this country alone gave over nine million dollars to the cause. All the principal heathen countries of the world are now penetrated by the missions of Christianity. At this moment, over China, India, Japan, Persia, Hindustan, Turkey, Bulgaria, Africa, Madagascar, Greenland, and the hundreds of Pacific isles, there are over forty thousand Christian laborers toiling diligently to represent unto guilty and sorrowful men the glory, the beauty, and the healing of Christ's love. In these lands schools, colleges, and theological seminaries have been established, wherein Christian education is given to more than one million youths of both sexes. Outside the bounds of Christendom there are now established at least four thousand centers of Christian teaching and living; more than three thousand Christian congregations have been gathered; over seven hundred thousand persons are now members of the Christian Church, while its nominal adherents reach into the millions. In India and Burmah alone, there are eight thousand missionaries, native preachers, and catechists; nearly three thousand stations and out-stations; more than seventy thousand communicants. The Baptists have made the Karens of Burmah a Christian people; the American Board has done the same for the Sandwich Islands; the Moravians for Greenland; the Wesleyans for the Fiji and Friendly Isles, and the English Independents for Madagascar. Consider those large and flourishing Christian Churches, born out of the very abysses of heathenism, in Australia, British America, the Sandwich Islands, Northern Turkey, Persia, China, Madagascar, South Africa, Liberia, Sierra Leone, and the islands of the Pacific. The largest church in the world, numbering four thousand five hundred members, is in Hilo, on the island of Hawaii, not yet fifty years removed from the most debased savagism. Over ninety thousand Fijians gather regularly for Sabbath worship, who, within thirty years, feasted on human flesh. In 1860 Madagascar had only a few hundred scattered and persecuted converts. Now the rulers of that land, with more than two hundred thousand of their subjects, are adherents of Christianity. During this century, in more than three hundred islands of Eastern and Southern Polynesia, the Gospel has swept heathenism entirely away. Ought not these facts to quicken our zeal, inflame our love, confirm our faith?

In the year 1760, in a room in Geneva, Switzerland, Voltaire boastingly predicted that "before the beginning of the nineteenth century, Christianity will have disappeared from the earth." William Carey was not born until one year later, but the missionary spirit which was born of his holy zeal has filled the century with the glorious record of its triumphs! Since the beginning of this century Protestantism alone has established hundreds of foreign mission stations, it has gathered an army of lay helpers numbering more than 35,000, it counts its communicants by the hundred thousand, and its nominal adherents by the million! In less than eighty years over 160,000,000 copies, in whole or in part, of the word of God have been scattered abroad—a number "thirty times as great as existed in all the previous thirty-three centuries since the law was given on Mount Sinai." The very room in which Voltaire uttered his vain prophecy is now a Bible depository, while the glorious Gospel of Christ, gathering to itself all increments of power, strong in the irresistible might of God, goes forth conquering and to conquer, until the whole earth shall rejoice in his salvation!

> "Watchman, tell us of the night;
>   Higher yet that star ascends.
> Traveler, blessedness and light,
>   Peace and truth, its course portends!
> Watchman, will its beams alone
>   Gild the spot that gave them birth!
> Traveler, ages are its own,
>   SEE, IT BURSTS O'ER ALL THE EARTH!"

THE GREAT KING IN DISGUISE.

Then came Jesus forth, wearing the crown of thorns, and the purple robe. And Pilate saith unto them, Behold the man!—John xix, 5.

IN the days of the Augustan empire, it was the custom of the Roman governors of Judea annually to release a prisoner to the people at the time of the Passover feast. Pontius Pilate sought to shield himself behind this precedent in his temporizing and cowardly effort to escape from a plain duty. In his fatal and guilty perplexity, he invited the people to ask him to release unto them the prisoner at his judgment seat, Jesus, the King of the Jews. Pilate found, as all men of like character find sooner or later to their cost, that, when face to face with a clear and undisputed duty, hesitation, indirection, evasive and circuitous courses lead to deeper entanglements and greater sin, for at once the crowd, instigated by the eager and wily priests and scribes, cried, saying, "Not this man, but Barabbas. Now Barabbas was a robber."

Then it was that the supreme indignity and cruelty of a Roman scourging was inflicted on Jesus. As their manner was, he was stripped to the waist, and tied to a pillar or post in a stooping posture, and was beaten by the pitiless soldiers with a cord of knotted rope or of plated leather thongs, armed at the end with sharp pieces of bone or small jagged drops of lead. It not unfrequently happened that the unfortunate victim perished while undergoing this horrible torture, or sank insensible before his tormentors, a scarcely recognizable mass of bruised, bleeding, quivering flesh. However much our reverence and love would incline us to hope the contrary, we may be sure that the full quota of stripes was laid upon the body of Jesus, for Jewish prisoners were specially distasteful to Roman soldiers, and his refusal to make any answer to the governor concerning the accusations brought against him would tend still further to exasperate the brutal guards. The cruel act completed, the rough, unfeeling legionaries led the stooping, bleeding Victim into the great hall of the governor's house, and, remembering that he had been called a king, they threw over him a faded soldier's cloak, sometimes of scarlet, sometimes of purple, as a rude burlesque of the rich and splendid purple one worn by the Roman emperors. With some twigs of the thorny Nubk bush, growing hard by, they improvised a mock laurel-wreath like that worn on public occasions by the Cæsars, and pressed down its close, sharp thorns on his temples, the blood meanwhile trickling down his face! They forced into his trembling hand a long reed, in mockery of the scepters held by kings, and then they gave full vent to their grim and awful humor. They kneeled before him in derision, saying, "Hail, King of the Jews." Then they took the reed from his hand and smote him on the face and head, and as well with the palms of their hands, while some, indulging their coarse contempt to the full, spit upon him. Thus they mocked and scorned and jeered and derided him, until even their violence and brutality finally wore itself out, and during it all the divine Sufferer murmured not, nor spake a single word. The depth and patience and majesty of his solitary anguish seems to have touched the stern heart of Pilate, for, seeing him thus, he determined to make one more effort to save his life. He went forth again to the fierce, angry, vengeful crowd, ordering Jesus at the same time to be brought forth with him, wearing the scarlet cloak, crowned with thorns, covered with the vile proofs of contempt and violence, and tottering with extreme pain and weakness. "Behold, I bring him before you once more. The scourging has not extorted a single word of confession from him. I find no fault in him at all." And then, as though he would appeal to their compassion, he said, "Behold the Man?" And what did they behold? A figure bent by the scourging, invested with the garments and insignia of mock royalty, a pale, worn, and bleeding face—the thorn-crowned Man of sorrows! And what did the angels behold? What did they behold who dwell in the overhanging spiritual realm, their eyes so purged from earthly grossness as that they may see the course and issues of the eternal realities? They saw the Son of the Highest, by the word of whose power the worlds are upheld, and in virtue of whom all things consist, meekly enduring all this scorn and contumely and mockery and insult, giving the uttermost proof of his holy and tender love for men, the light of the knowledge of the glory of God shining in his face, and the vast dominion of the unending ages stretching away in resplendent glory before him!

But the pathetic spectacle moved not to mercy or pity his fierce and unrelenting persecutors. They were hounding him to the death. Their thirst was for blood. They were priests, and priestly cruelty, like the grave, is cold, hard, pitiless, insatiable. The greedy blood-hunger of a fanatical and persecuting priesthood, no more than the ravenous grave, has ever yet, in any time or land, said, "Enough, enough!" Religious hate is a passion easily aroused, but when once it has gained the complete control of a man, a sect, or a party it can be effectually laid only by the strong, resistless hand of Almighty God. "When the chief priests therefore and the officers saw him, they cried out, saying, Crucify him, crucify him."

1. As Pilate to these Jews, so God perpetually, by various voices, is saying to every man born in a Christian land, trained amid Christian influences, "Behold the Man!" Whether we will or no, we must hear that voice, we must look at the great King in disguise. In childhood, in youth, in vigorous manhood, in halting age, in every period and circumstance of life, it speaks to our hearts. We cannot drown that Voice, we cannot hide that Face, from our eyes. Hear we must, look we

must, until the last choice is made by which we elect our spiritual, eternal destiny. We may fill our eyes with other visions, the strife and clamor and din of the world may seal our ears against the celestial voices, but there will be times, occasions, experiences when this voice will strangely hush all other sounds, and we will hear distinctly and solemnly the penetrating words, " Behold the Man!" We may not choose to look upon this worn and bleeding face, we may even strive to put far from us the visage that was marred more than the sons of men, but there will be hours when all visions of splendor and beauty and pleasure and power and ambition and wealth will be swept clean away, and between our souls and eternity nothing will remain but the Man of sorrows appealing for our love and obedience.

2. As with these Jews, so with us, we must accept him as our King, or reject him, and send him to the cross. One of the accusations brought against him was, " He makes himself a King." Yes, he is a King. To the Jews a false king; to the Romans a mock king, but to us he is, and must forever remain, a real King. As we behold him, shall we accept him? A King we must have, *will* have, DO have. The question is not, Shall we have a King? but, Who shall be our King? Known by various names are the kings that rule men, but every man, first and last, owns a king. It may be pleasure, or ambition, or wealth, or power, but something we do have. Is he not a worthy King? Is he not our

only worthy King? He stood there a King, the King of his own spirit and life and kingdom. Contrast him with Pilate and the Jews. They were slaves, hirelings, cowards. Was he not a real King?

The postponement of his claims is equivalent to a temporary rejection of them. What is it but the spirit and purpose on our part to serve one or the other of these false kings for a season, and at our own leisure to turn and embrace the service of the true King?

Christ is sent to the cross every time men reject him when he is truly and persuasively presented to them. Who are his crucifiers? Who are they who send him to the cross? They who are satisfied to live the life of grossness, baseness, sordidness, selfishness, and the malign passions of the mind, and to refuse the life of obedience, penitence, faith, and love.

3. There is that in the nature and life and offices of this thorn-crowned King which should commend him to our deepest reverence and strongest faith, our holiest love, and our unfaltering obedience. "Behold the Man!" What does Pilate say? "I find no fault in him!" Who has found any fault in him? Who convinceth him of sin? He is holy, harmless, undefiled, separate from sinners. He is absolutely without spot or blemish. Shall we not be drawn by this spectacle of flawless, spotless, radiant purity? Is it so common that we can afford to despise him?

"Behold the Man!" The law of duty was the

law of his life. "I came not to do my own will, but the will of him that sent me." "My meat is to do the will of him that sent me." "I must work the works of him that sent me, while it is day: the night cometh, when no man can work." "IT is finished." Ought not this to be the law of every life? Has life any significance, any force, any beauty, without it? Is not this complete surrender to duty rare and glorious?

"Behold the Man!" He bore quiet, faithful, unflinching testimony to the truth. "To this end was I born, and for this cause came I into the world, that I should bear witness unto the truth." Consider the kind of truth to which he bore witness. Not local, temporary, institutional truth, but spiritual, necessary, universal, eternal truth. And is not this a grand office, to bear witness to the truth? The admiration we feel for the truth-speaker in any sphere is spontaneous and sincere. His witness may be a very humble one, it may be for a merely local, typical, temporary truth, but we weave a chaplet of honor for him who sees it and utters it. How much more for him who was and is THE TRUTH!

"Behold the Man!" How meekly and calmly and sublimely does he hold his vast and mighty powers in reserve? He is thorn-crowned. His hands are weak and pulseless, and the long reed trembles as he barely supports it. His pierced flesh quivers with agony, the blood drops from his brows. His brain throbs with pain, his heart is breaking with the burden of its great, mysterious sorrow. And why is he so defenseless? Is it because he is weaker than his enemies? A word from him, and as lightning—smiting, scorching—leaps from the bosom of the black cloud the secret fires would shrivel them up before his face. A single wave of his hand, and the earth would open and swallow them up. Those mute lips, let them but move in prayer to his Father, and instantly twelve legions of armed angels would flame about him. All power is his, in heaven and on earth, but he will use it only for lofty and glorious spiritual ends. It is a sacred and charmed deposit, and he will never use it for himself, for his own protection and sustenance, or for the purposes of vainglory, as tempted to do in the wilderness. That power is for others: to relieve pain and suffering, to feed, to clothe, to solace, to heal—and to bless, to forgive and sanctify and beautify the penitent and aspiring soul. He suffers, but not in his own right, not on his own account, not for himself, but for us; the just for the unjust, that he might bring us to God.

Behold him as your Guide. Do you not need a guide? Are you never perplexed? Have you no experience of conflict of duties? Behold him as your Friend, faithful, delicate, sympathizing, all-powerful. Do you not yearn for such a friend? Is not your heart hungry for such wealth and delicacy and fidelity of love as he only can give? Behold him as your present, gracious, patient, complete Saviour.

4. The Jews scornfully, contemptuously rejected

him, and their ruin was swift, complete, inevitable; so with every soul that willfully puts him away. No life is in danger with Christ; every life is in peril without him. The clear, open, complete disclosure of Christ to a human soul is to that soul the beginning of spiritual life or death, as Christliness is every-where heaven, and selfishness is every-where hell.

Behold, I bring him forth before you. The soldiers have worked their will upon him. "Behold the Man!" What will you do with him? Will you mock him? Will you deride him? Will you kneel in mock solemnity, saying, "Hail, King of the Jews?" Will you smite him? Will you cry, "Crucify him?" This was the third time Pilate brought him before these Jews. He has been in your presence before. You have said, "He is not my King." Will you say it again? You have smitten him in the face with your refusals. Will you smite him again? You have said, "Let him go to the cross, I will go my way." Will you say it again?

"Behold the Man!" Mock him no more. Smite him no more. Give him to the crucifiers no more. Cry out with Thomas, "My Lord and my God!" Accept him as your Brother, Saviour, King, and he will bless and honor and exalt you for evermore!

THE PROPHETIC VISION OF GOD.

Philip saith unto him, Lord, show us the Father, and it sufficeth us. Jesus saith unto him, Have I been so long time with you, and yet hast thou not known me, Philip? He that hath seen me hath seen the Father; and how sayest thou then, Show us the Father?—John xiv, 8-9.

Two things are necessary in order to the production of a result in a moral agent. First, a perceiving, recipient, and responsive faculty; and, second, a truth adapted to awaken, arouse, gratify, or feed that faculty. Two things are necessary in order to vision: light and the eye. Two things are necessary in order to respiration: air and lungs. Two things are necessary in order to the production of hearing: an ear and sound. Whenever there is light and an eye there must be vision; whenever there is air and lungs there must be respiration. It is not a question of volition at all. Given an open eye and light, and the will has nothing to do with the matter. Vision follows without any determination on the part of the will. It does not require an effort of volition in order to hear when there is sound and a ear; it follows without volition. So there are sensibilities, emotions, capacities in man which are excited without any reference to the will, and there are some faculties, some susceptibilities in the human spirit whose activity cannot in any wise be determined by the will. A man cannot make himself glad when he is sad simply by resolving to be glad. You cannot by an effort of the will compel yourself to love that which is inherently unlovely, or to recognize as superior that which is confessedly inferior. Yonder on the public square is a veiled statue; the hour has arrived for its public display; at a given signal the shroud falls away. It is hideous! It is misshapen! It is distorted! It is any thing but a sight of beauty! Now, no amount of argument on the part of the sculptor, however gifted he may be, can prove to you that an ugly and hideous statue is a thing of grace and proportion, and your will cannot make that appear beautiful which is intrinsically ugly. We cannot believe that love is hate. We may indeed say that it is, with our lips. But I am not talking about lips; I am talking about the actual feeling, the real response of one's soul. We cannot make love appear to the mind as an identical quality with hate. We cannot make truth and a lie the same thing to our spirits. We cannot make that which is repulsive seem fair and lovely.

These are the underlying principles, the basal truths, of all true, enduring spiritual philosophy, and any religion that aspires to universal sway and permanent authority among men must have respect to these principles. No religion can ever come to permanent authority, no religion can ever come to universal sway, that does not root itself in, and propagate itself by, a devout and honest and straightforward recognition of these truths.

"Thou shalt love the Lord thy God with all thy heart, and with all thy might, and with all thy soul, and with all thy strength." It is taken for granted in this commandment that God is worthy of such a love. The underlying assumption is that he is a Being fitted to call forth that kind of love; and if he is not, the mere command to love him does not make it right. It is not right to love God just because we are commanded to love him. It is not right to love any superior being just because we are ordered to do so. We must not, yea, we cannot, really love any being, stronger than ourselves, simply by virtue of a command. If that being is unjust, if that being is cruel, if that being is unrighteous, it may be our duty not to love him; and the righteousness of loving God does not consist in merely obeying an outward command to love him. It consists in our capacity to recognize the lovable qualities in him. Therefore it is the supreme duty of the Christian religion, inasmuch as it commands men on the pain and penalty of eternal death to love God—it is, I say, the duty of the Christian religion to see to it that it shall present God as worthy of such love. I will not worship a demon just because at some time or other some religious fanatic calls him God. I will not do violence to my moral nature just because some ignorant zealot tells me that I must fall down and worship any being who is stronger than I am. No man can love a devil just because some superstitious recluse calls him God. There may be times, there have been times, in the religious history of the world when it was the instant duty of all good and right-minded men not to love the Being that was put forth as God. It is, and I repeat it with reverence, the first duty of Christianity, commanding men as it does to yield to the divine Being supreme and passionate affection—an affection that absorbs the whole nature—it is the duty of this religion to see to it that the Supreme Being shall be presented to men as worthy of their love.

Have you ever studied the contents of the prophetic vision of God? Have you ever taken the Old Testament Scriptures and carefully inquired into the kind of a God these old Hebrew seers foretold? It is remarkable how they not only predicted the coming of a great Person, the coming of a strange and wonderful Being, but how they almost always so phrased their predictions as to bring prominently to the fore the truth that God, as he shall be disclosed to the world through Israel, should be presented as an attractive, winning, drawing, magnetic Being.

Let me read you some passages of Scripture in order to justify this statement. The pith and marrow, the inner heart and spirit, of all these passages is that there should come from the peculiar and chosen people such a disclosure of the divine nature as would draw men to it: "The scepter shall not depart from Judah, nor a lawgiver from between his feet, until Shiloh come; and unto him shall the gathering of the people be." There is not a hint here of the use of force to bring the people to Shiloh.

There is not the faintest suggestion of the employment of coercion. So far from there being any thing in Shiloh to repel people, the dying Jacob predicted that the people should gather about him as steel filings about a magnet. "Behold, thou shalt call a nation that thou knowest not, and nations that knew not thee shall run unto thee, because of the Lord thy God, and for the Holy One of Israel; for he hath glorified thee." Through, by means of, the Jewish nation a new unfolding of the divine nature is be expected, and such shall be its beauty that other nations, hearing of it, should run unto Israel because of the Lord their God. "And it shall come to pass in the last days, that the mountain of the Lord's house shall be established in the top of the mountains, and shall be exalted above the hills; and all nations shall flow unto it. And many people shall go and say, Come ye, and let us go up to the mountain of the Lord, to the house of the God of Jacob; and he will teach us of his ways, and we will walk in his paths." Is not that in outline a description of a God who would draw people to him? "And in that day there shall be a root of Jesse, which shall stand for an ensign of the people; to it shall the Gentiles seek." If there are any soldiers here, they know that wherever the ensign is on the field of battle, that is where they are to seek, and there is to be such a disclosure of God in Christ Jesus that what the colors are to soldiers on the field of battle, God, as seen in Christ, is to be to the nations. "And the inhabitants of one city shall go to another, saying,

Let us go speedily to pray before the Lord, and to seek the Lord of hosts: I will go also. Yea, many people and strong nations shall come *to seek* the Lord of hosts in Jerusalem, and to pray before the Lord."

My object in reading these passages from the Old Testament has been to show that the final disclosure of God, according to the contents of the Hebrew prophecy, was to be the disclosure of a Being of irresistible drawing power, of irresistible spiritual magnetism, and to show that, my language was not too strong when I said that, if men are to love God with all their hearts, it is the duty of the teachers of Christianity to see that they shall present to men a God worthy of love. Clearly it was the expectation of the Hebrew prophets that such a God should be manifested to men by the coming of their Messiah.

Have the teachers of Christianity always done it? Bishop Foster, speaking elsewhere, protected by years and scholarship and eminent ability, could say that Christianity has suffered more from the errors of its friends than the malice of its foes. If I may not make this statement as an original one, I may at least quote it from the eminent and godly Bishop, and strongly emphasize its truth. For it is true that Christianity has suffered more from the errors of its friends than the malice of its foes. Was that God who was declared to men from the eighth to the sixteenth century of the Christian era, a God calculated to win and draw people? Was he calculated to attract the admiration, win the homage, and call forth the affections of strong and noble natures? That God who was represented as delighting in nothing so much as the eternal burning of heretics; that God who had committed the distribution of his mercies into the hands of a few Italian priests, with their head-quarters on the banks of the Tiber; that God who permitted these priests freely to dispense and dispose of his mercy, whose sins they remitted being remitted, whose sins they refused to forgive being still binding; that God who damned men for opinions, not for conduct; that God who was declared to be pleased with the sight of human beings in exquisite pain—was that God worthy of the supreme love of noble hearts? No! a thousand times, No! He was worthy of universal execration.

Two or three years ago I read, in a monthly magazine sent to a great many preachers in this country, the following words from an eminent divine, an eminent Protestant divine, a clergyman of one of the most influential and highly cultured religious bodies in the United States: "Tone up the pew to the cordial acceptance of every article of our Confession. The sound conservatism of the New England heart, and the New England head, and the old New England piety will, I trust, erelong, by the grace of God, bring back the theology of New England to the platform of Jonathan Edwards and the fathers." Well, I thought I would see about this matter a little, and find out just what kind of a Confession it was that the pew was to be toned up to in every article.

I found it. Here is a single specimen of its gracious utterance: "By the decree of God, for the manifestation of his glory, some men and angels are predestined unto everlasting life, and others are fore-ordained to everlasting death. These angels and men, thus predestined and fore-ordained, are particularly and unchangeably designed, and their number is so certain and definite that it cannot be either increased or diminished. The rest of mankind God was pleased, according to the unsearchable counsel of his own self, whereby he extendeth or withholdeth mercy as he pleaseth, for the glory of his sovereign power over his creatures, to pass by, and to ordain them to dishonor and wrath for their sin, to the praise of his glorious justice." Do you wonder that doubters and infidels are as plentiful in New England as they are said to be? I wonder that they are not all infidels, in the presence of such teaching concerning God. Am I to be commanded to love the God who, sitting in the solitude and calmness of eternity, ere yet any world had been created, should deliberately preconceive the whole plan of this creation, who foresaw all that would happen, and deliberately filled the earth with beings who are ordained to sin that they might suffer, and then in wrath appointed to eternal suffering? Men may through fear say with their lips that they love such a God, but they no more love him than they love a devil. Nor is this all. "The sound conservatism of the New England heart, and the New England head, and the old New England piety will, I trust, erelong, by the grace of God, bring back the theology of New England to the platform of Jonathan Edwards and the fathers." Several years ago, I invested in Jonathan Edwards's works. He was a very great and holy and godly man, but he was not pope, thank God! He preached a great many sermons, and one of the most famous of them is entitled, "Sinners in the Hands of an Angry God." Let me read to you a specimen of the old-fashioned theology of Jonathan Edwards, to which we are soon to return. In this sermon on "Sinners in the Hands of an Angry God," preached to those whom he styles "the unregenerate," he says: "The God that holds you over the pit of hell, much as one holds a spider, or some loathsome insect, over the fire, abhors you, and is dreadfully provoked; his wrath toward you burns like fire; he looks upon you as worthy of nothing else, but to be cast into the fire; he is of purer eyes than to bear to have you in his sight; you are ten thousand times so abominable in his sight as the most hateful and venomous serpent is in ours." "Consider this, you that are here present, that yet remain in an unregenerate state. That God will execute the fierceness of his anger implies that he will inflict wrath without any pity." Now if, in a fit of anger, I should correct my child *without any pity*, and it should become generally known, this whole Church would speedily ask for a new pastor. And yet we are asked to bow down and worship a God who will deliberately inflict pain on his wayward children, without any pity! "When God beholds the ineffable extremity of your case, and sees your torment so vastly disproportioned to your strength, and sees how your poor soul is crushed and sinks down, as it were, into an infinite gloom, he will have no compassion upon you, he will not forbear the executions of his wrath, or in the least lighten his hand; there shall be no moderation or mercy, nor will God then at all stay his rough wind; he will have no regard to your welfare, nor be at all careful lest you should suffer too much, in any other sense than only that you should not suffer beyond what strict justice requires; nothing should be withheld." Mark the language! There is nothing more terrific in Dante's Inferno or Milton's hell. "Nothing shall be withheld because it is so hard for you to bear." Once more: "Thus it will be with you that are in an unconverted state, if you continue in it; the infinite might and majesty and terribleness of the omnipotent God shall be magnified upon you in the ineffable strength of your torments; you shall be tormented in the presence of the holy angels, and in the presence of the Lamb; and when you shall be in this state of suffering, the glorious inhabitants of heaven shall go forth and look on the awful spectacle, that they may see what the wrath and fierceness of the Almighty is; and when they have seen it, they will fall down and adore that great power and majesty."

And then I am asked to account for the prevalence and spread of modern infidelity! There is nothing difficult in accounting for the infidelity of any man who has been brought up to believe in the

existence of such a God. He is not the God of the
Bible; he is not the God of the New Testament;
he is not the God whom we are commanded to love
with all our heart and mind and soul and strength.
He is a heated, barbaric, mediæval invention, worthy
of the worship only of those who cower and cringe,
and are servile and cowardly. Not by the worship
of such a God will men ever be redeemed from sinfulness and cowardice and cruelty. If God in heaven
can exhaust the full tide of his power and wrath upon
his own lost children; if in heaven, with a heart like
flint or marble or stone, God may look upon his
sinning children, and no tears ever bedim the infinite
Father's eye as the endless procession of lost souls
goes down to eternal night, then how do you ask
me to pity my child when he goes wrong? How
do you ask me to weep tears of sorrow over the loss
of my son or daughter, if God takes with perfect indifference the loss, the eternal ruin, of the majority
of the children he has made? No! No! No! Before the reasonable intelligence of this time, before
the sweet spirit of Christian love that is now abroad
in the world, such a cruel and wicked conception
of God is doomed to die. May the day of its death
hasten!

"Show us the Father, and it sufficeth us." Who
is God? I mean, who is the Christian God? Not,
who is Jupiter; not, who is Thor; not, who is the
God of the Italian priests on the banks of the Tiber;
not, who is this God that regales heaven by leading
its inhabitants to the outer battlements that they

may joyously witness the torments of hell; but, who is the God of Jesus Christ? *He* himself is. "He that hath seen ME hath seen the Father." And who and what kind of a God is that? He is the God into whose presence a company of sneering, jeering Pharisees pushed and jostled and thrust a guilty woman, with burning face, and then in pious horror stood aloof, as if to say: "There! look at that thing; we caught her in the very act! Moses in the law said we should stone such to death. Now, what do *you* say?" Willing to expose and put to public shame this poor, wretched creature, if only they could entrap him! And he stooped down and wrote in the sand, and said: "Let him that is without fault among you cast the first stone." And again he stooped down and began to write, while they, beginning with the eldest, went out one after another, until Infinite Purity was left alone with human weakness, guilt, and crime. "Where are those thine accusers?" "No man, Lord." "Neither do I condemn thee: go, and sin no more." I bow my knee to HIM; I give my heart to HIM; I will follow HIS guidance as long as I live; I will not fear to commit my soul to HIM when I die. See, yonder is a funeral procession slowly winding about the wall of the city, seeking the burial-place of the dead. There is one mourner only; she is a widow; the dead man is her only son. And he, coming toward the city, meets the sad procession, and without paying any attention apparently to the dead man, looks upon her, and "has compassion" on her;

and then in pity he brings back to life her son and her hope. He is ascending the side of Olivet, and the golden pinnacles of the splendid temple flash before him, and he stops and says: "O Jerusalem, Jerusalem, thou that killest the prophets, and stonest them that are sent unto thee; how oft would I have gathered thy children together, as a hen gathereth her brood under her wings, but ye would not! Behold, your house is left unto you desolate."

Who is our God? See that father coming yonder with the dumb idiot boy; he foams at the mouth; he is torn, he raves, and throws himself violently on the ground. The poor, broken-hearted father had brought him to his disciples, and they could do nothing for him. He brings him now to the Master, and as he approaches him he throws himself on the ground, and wallows, foaming! And Jesus stops and says: "How long ago since this came to him?" "Since he was a child; and ofttimes it casts him into water; and into the fire. If thou canst do any thing, help us." And Jesus says: "All things are possible to him that believeth." The father, through his tears, cries out, "Lord, I believe; help thou mine unbelief." "I charge thee, thou deaf and dumb spirit, come out of him;" and he restored him whole to his father! This is our God! On Sunday he goes into a synagogue in Capernaum. The holy people are there; the people who imagine that God has given into their special keeping his holy day and the government of this part of the universe. They are there who would pull their sheep or ass

The Prophetic Vision of God. 171

out of the pit very quickly, and here is a man with a withered arm; and they wait, and watch to see if Jesus will heal him on the Sabbath day. "And he saith, Stretch forth thy hand. And he stretched it forth, and immediately it was whole like the other." Jesus, who sent special word to John that the poor have the Gospel preached unto them; Jesus, who fulfilled in himself the ancient prophecy that he would not quench the smoking flax or break the bruised reed; Jesus, who, had he but spoken, could in an instant of time have caused the whole earth, with all its populations, to have disappeared forever, but who instead went meekly to the cross, and patiently bore all its mysterious suffering, and has thus taught us that strength is to mother weakness, that riches are to feed poverty, that genius is to serve ignorance, that holiness is to cleanse guilt, that the life and health of the universe are secured by the sacrificial love of God—who would not love and serve him! And he is God, for "he that hath seen me, hath seen the Father!" In this truth, let us live; by this truth, let us work and suffer and be patient; and by this truth we need not fear to die!

> " Who fathoms the eternal thought?
>   Who talks of scheme and plan?
> The Lord is God, he needeth not
>   The poor device of man.
>
> " I see the wrong that round me lies,
>   I feel the guilt within,
> I hear, with groan and travail cries,
>   The world confess its sin.

"Yet in the maddening maze of things,
  And tossed by storm and flood,
To one fixed stake my spirit clings;
  I know that God is good!

"And so beside the silent sea
  I wait the muffled oar;
No harm from him can come to me,
  On ocean or on shore."

THE BRAVE CHOICE OF MOSES.

By faith Moses, when he was come to years, refused to be called the son of Pharaoh's daughter; choosing rather to suffer affliction with the people of God, than to enjoy the pleasures of sin for a season; esteeming the reproach of Christ greater riches than the treasures in Egypt: for he had respect unto the recompense of the reward.—Heb. xi, 24-26.

THE life of Moses began amid obscure and perilous surroundings. He was a slave child in an ancient Oriental despotism, and a more unpromising beginning, a sadder, harder, more pitiless fate, it would be impossible to conceive. He was born at a time when the fortunes of his people touched their lowest point, for just prior to his birth Pharaoh had issued the murderous edict commanding every male Hebrew child as soon as born to be destroyed by drowning. The strangely mingled love, faith, and cunning of his parents combined to save him for three months from the curious, prying, inquisitorial eyes of the Egyptian emissaries. When, however, concealment was no longer possible, they hastily fashioned the crude ark of bulrushes, daubed it without and within with slime and pitch, placed the goodly boy-babe therein, and laid it in the flags by the river's brink. They turned away doubtless with tears and prayers, but they did not forget to station hard by the quick-witted little Miriam, so that she could observe the fate of the ark and its precious occupant, and be enabled speedily to report to her parents. I will not attempt to trace in order the various events in this remarkable life leading up to the emergency of the text, when we find Moses making the brave and momentous choice whereby he should be forever enrolled among the heroes of God. You all know how the daughter of Pharaoh, Thermuthis by name, as tradition reports, going down to the river to bathe, observed the child, and sent her maid to fetch it; you remember how when she opened the ark the babe began to cry, and she had "compassion on him;" how suddenly Miriam glides into the presence of the princess, looking up into her face with perfect demureness; of her inimitable *naïveté* as she proposes to find a nurse for the crying baby among the Hebrew women; of how thus his own mother becomes his nurse; the princess adopting the foundling as her own son, calling him Moses, "for," she said, "I drew him out of the water."

Moses grew to manhood in the court of Egypt, at that time the most splendid and luxurious court in the whole world—a place not specially calculated to draw forth and strengthen the sterner and more robust moral virtues. At the court he was treated as became the son of the daughter of the king. *How* we know not; but when he came to years, that is, when he was grown up, or, literally, "when he became great," he found out in some way whose son he was; what blood actually flowed in his veins;

his relationship to those swarthy Hebrews, broiling in the sun yonder, mixing mortar and molding brick. What a revolution in his feelings! What days of separation, of meditation, and of loneliness must have followed the discovery. We can readily imagine the character of his thoughts and feeling during this time. The result was the heroic determination to confess his real kinship with these slaves, and share their dismal fortunes.

The sacrifice involved, and the complete change in his plans, associations, and ambitions that must necessarily have followed his decision, it is not necessary that we formally unfold. There were many inducements and solicitations on the side of the suppression of the facts. If he would only quietly consent to be called the son of Pharaoh's daughter, see what desirable things were his—at once and always! Riches, ease, pleasure, power, knowledge, ambition, every thing for eye and ear, and taste, and desire, for the body and the mind. On the other side, what were there? Poverty, toil, obscurity, self-denial, self-sacrifice, pain, and suffering—the closing up against him of every avenue of pleasure, power, fame, wealth, and ambition. Was not this a trying position for a young man? To a young man, the things he renounced were peculiarly inviting, seductive, and fascinating, and the things he chose proportionately forbidding, abhorrent, and repellent. The noble sonnet by which Lowell commemorated the noble choice and rare self-renunciation of Wendell Phillips applies with equal if not greater aptness, beauty, and force to the glorious and lofty choice of Moses:

> " He stood upon the world's broad threshold : wide
>   The din of battle and of slaughter rose ;
> He saw God stand upon the weaker side,
>   That sank in seeming loss before its foes ;
> Many there were who made great haste and sold
>   Unto the cunning enemy their swords.
> He scorned their gifts of fame and power and gold,
>   And, underneath their soft and flowery words,
> Heard the cold serpent hiss ; therefore he went
>   And humbly joined him to the weaker part,
> Fanatic named, and fool, yet well content,
>   So he could be the nearer to God's heart,
> And feel its solemn pulses sending blood
> Through all the wide-spread veins of endless good."

Where are we to look for the explanation, the secret inspiration, of this conduct of Moses? It is unusual, exceptional, extraordinary. There are not many men like Phillips and Moses. What secret power enabled him to choose as he did? First, and chiefly, FAITH inspired, directed, and sustained the choice. "By faith, Moses when he was come to years, refused to be called the son of Pharaoh's daughter." Faith is that power of the soul by which we apprehend the invisible, by which we see things, qualities, facts, realities, not disclosed to the ordinary eye. It gives us realities, not semblances; the permanent, not the fleeting ; the future, not the present ; the real, not the seeming; the moral, not the physical; the spiritual, not the secular; the eternal, and not the temporal. This power Moses pos-

The Brave Choice of Moses.

sessed to an extraordinary degree. He saw ordinary things with his eyes just as other men saw them—the palace, the pleasant gardens along the Nile, the ease, the wealth, the luxury—he saw all those things, but he saw with the eyes of his soul far more than he saw with the eyes of his body. He had pierced the visible and seized the invisible. He saw things as they were, and not as they seemed to be. He knew, indeed, whose son he was: not the son of Pharaoh's daughter, nor of the swarthy Hebrews of the tribe of Levi, but the son of God; the son of duty, of truth, of right. He saw how fleeting, how unsubstantial, how unsatisfying, how base and ignoble were the pleasures of sin, of mere sense and appetite, as compared with the peace and power that follow the soul's obedience to the higher law. He knew who these Goshen slaves were, too: God's chosen people, and that of them a King should arise with a nobler rule than earth ever knew before, with a dominion wider and more enduring than the proudest Pharaoh might ever boast. These were some of the disclosures made to him by that supreme faculty of the spirit described as faith.

He was sustained and supported, too, by the conviction that there would come to him a fitting recompense, an ample and glorious reward. "He had respect unto the recompense of the reward." Not that he clearly foresaw the whole of the great work he was to do, and the splendid reward which should be his for doing it, but that he had that secret sense which all good and true men have that wherever in the wide universe one seeks to do the right he shall not miss of his reward. We can easily imagine what they thought and said of him about this time in the Egyptian court: "What a pity that such a splendid fellow should throw himself away!" "He is too squeamish. He stands too much on trifles." It seems that about this time Mr. and Mrs. They-Say were on a visit to the Egyptian court. "Foolish fellow," they say, "he is throwing away every thing." "He is following a mere sentiment. He is a mere idle dreamer." Threw away every thing? He gained every thing! First of all, he gained a lofty sense of self-respect, without which no man is ever good, or strong, or great. Nor can we really respect ourselves until we do something great—something that makes us feel that we have in us the stuff out of which heroes and saints are made, something really grand and noble. Moses must have felt this kindling inspiration on that day when he walked out of the palace, never once turning to look back at the splendor and glories he was leaving, his face headed toward the brick-kilns and toiling slaves of Goshen. "He had respect unto the recompense of the reward."

"For he had respect unto the recompense of the reward." What do mine eyes see? Behold! the Son of man suddenly transfigured before them! His face shines as the sun, and his garments are white as the light. And what else do I see? "And, behold, there appeared MOSES and Elias talking with him." Moses had respect unto the recompense of the reward. Consider his vast and colossal place and power in human history. Contrast with his the proudest names in Greek and Roman history. The position of Moses, as the son of Pharaoh's daughter, must have appeared to the court people at the time as one of the first in the whole world. Little did they know of the real truth in the matter. The name of what Pharaoh, yea, or what dozen Pharaohs, is to be mentioned along-side of the name of Moses now?

Consider his funeral—the grandest ever given to man. The Lord himself buried him there in a valley in the land of Moab.

> " But when the warrior dieth
>   His comrades in the war,
> With arms reversed and muffled drum,
>   Follow the funeral car.
> They show the banners taken,
>   They tell his battles won,
> And after him lead his masterless steed,
>   While peals the minute gun.
>
> " Amid the noblest of the land
>   Men lay the sage to rest,
> And give the bard an honored place
>   With costly marble drest,
> In the great minster transept,
>   Where lights like glories fall,
> And the choir sings and the organ rings
>   Along the emblazoned wall.
>
> " This was the bravest warrior
>   That ever buckled sword ;
> This the most gifted poet
>   That ever breathed a word ;

And never earth's philosopher
  Traced with his golden pen
On the deathless page truth half so sage
  As he wrote down for men.

"And had he not high honor?
  The hill-side for his pall,
To lie in state while angels wait,
  With stars for tapers tall,
And the dark rock-pines like tossing plumes
  Over his bier to wave,
And God's own hand in the lonely land
  To lay him in the grave."

Higher than earthly honor has been accorded him. Once to a lonely exile, on a rugged isle of the Ægean Sea, the gates of the Eternal City were thrown open, and he saw as it were far adown its shining golden streets. He beheld somewhat of its mighty glory and triumph, he heard somewhat of its sublime symphony of joy and victory. And what do you think he saw, and what do you think he heard? Hear him: "And I saw as it were a sea of glass mingled with fire: and them that had gotten the victory over the beast, and over his image, and over his mark, and over the number of his name, stand on the sea of glass, having the harps of God. And they sing the song of MOSES, the servant of God, and the song of the Lamb, saying, Great and marvelous are thy works, Lord God Almighty; just and true are thy ways, thou King of saints!"

Let us now gather up some of the lessons of wisdom, bravery, success, and righteousness afforded us by this history.

The Brave Choice of Moses.

1. When young men come to years they are constrained to a solemn and most momentous choice. The earlier years of life are largely those of impression, instinct, inclination, impulse, desire. It is the time for pictures, dreams, ideals, sentiments, enthusiasms. Every thing is in a fluid, plastic state or condition. Into each life, however, there comes at last a period of "moral thoughtfulness," as Arnold of Rugby would style it. Its essence is that of Moses; that is, shall we be real, or only *seem* to be? Out of this experience issue those choices which determine the drift, the ends, the character of all that is to follow. What we are to do, what we are to get, what we are to achieve, and, above all, what we are *to be*, all depend upon the determinations of this early era of moral thoughtfulness. Such a crisis came to Moses. Such a crisis comes to every one of us—some of us are even now making our choices.

You have heard of the fabled choice of Hercules. When a young man, he goes out to a solitary place to muse upon his future course in life. Two female figures approach him; one in white apparel, with a noble countenance, open, innocent, inviting, the other loosely, almost wantonly attired, her face painted and bedizened, with a bold, forward air, and furtively glancing about her to see if people looked at her. As the two drew nearer, the latter ran hastily forward, and addressed Hercules with the greatest familiarity: "O Hercules, I see that you are in great perplexity about your future course in life. If you will follow me you shall have a smooth and charming road. You need not burden your mind with business, or battles, or work of any kind. Your entire study hereafter shall be where to find the best wines and the most tempting dishes, the sweetest odors and the most becoming clothes, the happiest companions and the merriest amusements. Nor need you take any trouble as to the means necessary to support this style of life, for certain friends and familiars of mine will see to it that you are liberally provided for in this direction." "And pray, madam," asked Hercules, "what might be your name?" "My real name is Pleasure, but certain of my enemies have nicknamed me Vice." I fancy that she must have blushed—if Vice ever does blush—and dropped her head, as she was giving her name.

Then in a quiet, serious, modest way spoke the other: "Hercules, I knew your parents; I have noted and observed your ways from boyhood, and I am sure you are capable of noble deeds; but I must not delude you with false promises. As the Higher Powers have arranged the world, you can hope for nothing good or desirable without work. If you would number the gods among your friends, you must serve them; if you would be loved by those about you, you must make yourself useful; if you want your field to be fruitful, you must till it; if you want to be honored by all Greece, you must render it some brave and illustrious service; if you wish to be a great warrior, you must take lessons from some good soldier; you must bring the body into subjection, and must in every thing submit to wise discipline." It was a frank, open statement, concealing nothing from the fresh, eager, impulsive spirit, but it won the heart of Hercules, and at once he rose up, and followed virtue along the path of duty and honor, and so became the renowned liberator of Greece. To a like choice, every young man here feels himself divinely impelled. Resist the solicitations of vice. Heed and obey the solemn commands of virtue and religion.

2. This choice, and all similar ones, involve straightforwardness, sincerity, and reality. If we carefully analyze this choice of Moses, if we go to the center of the matter at once, what do we find? Simply that Moses meant to be himself and not somebody else; to be true, open, manly, honest, sincere. He was not willing to be thought something other than he was, as, for example, the son of Pharaoh's daughter, when, in fact, he was the son of a Hebrew slavewoman. He would not sail under false colors! If we would imitate Moses in the essential spirit of his decision, we must inflexibly resolve never to appear other than we are.

3. The rewards of righteousness, if slow, are solid, substantial, and enduring, and we are to choose them, however distant they may seem, rather than the temporary pleasures of sin. They greatly err who talk as if sin had no pleasures. Consider those things within easy reach of Moses, and tell me

frankly if they were not peculiarly enticing and attractive, and especially to a young man. Ease, wealth, pleasure, power—while human nature remains what it is these things must be attractive to men. Sin has its pleasures; they are real, keen, zestful, but they are only for a season; the seeds of speedy death are in them. The path of righteousness is sometimes dangerous, sometimes dismal, sometimes lonely, sometimes without promise of success or reward. Let it be distinctly known that the way of virtue is always surrounded with difficulties, and sometimes is beset with perils. These may deter the indolent, the supine, the cowardly; but they are only so many bugle blasts to the earnest and the brave. The fruits of righteousness ripen slowly, but they ripen, and they are forever sweet and pleasant to the taste. Its rewards come gradually, but they come, *and they are abiding*. O, my young friends,

> "The path of duty IS the way to glory!
> He that walks it, only thirsting
> For the right, and learns to deaden
> Love of self, before his journey closes
> He shall find the stubborn thistle bursting
> Into glossy purples, which outredden
> All voluptuous garden-roses. . . .
> He that, ever, ever following her commands,
> On with toil of heart and knees and hands,
> Thro' the long gorge to the far light has won
> His path upward, and prevailed,
> Shall find the toppling crags of duty scaled
> Are close upon the shining table-lands
> To which our God himself is sun and moon."

4. We, no more than Moses, can come to power and success here without the blessed and glorious illuminations and inspirations of faith. The young man as he looks around him must see many tempting pleasures, and as he looks within his own heart and nature he discovers strong desires pleading for gratification. The enticements and allurements of the life of the flesh, of the present, of pleasure, are immediate, insinuating, numerous, and potent. Have you never heard the young man's strong plea for himself, as for the first time he looks upon the world of forbidden and tempting pleasures? This young man, Moses, might have urged a plea in his own behalf—how strong, how plausible, how natural, how nicely calculated to deceive! We need, as Moses needed, the power of faith. We will not make the present serve the future until we see that future to be greater than this present, and only faith can show us this. And so with all the other malign elements with which we are in conflict. There must come to us the quick insight, the far outlook, the firm and steady grasp of faith before we will be strong enough to renounce all the pleasures of sin, to embrace a life of self-denial and self-sacrifice, strong enough to denounce and fight the popular and profitable lie, strong enough "to dare to be in the right with two or three."

Here you stand, many of you, at the parting of the ways. There are two ways, let men say what they will. One is the right way, the other is the wrong way. There is a difference in the ways, *and you see it.* Choose you must. There is no evading it. You cannot stand there *forever, refusing to decide.* That is simply one method of choosing the wrong way. How will you choose? In the strife of truth with falsehood, once to every man upon this earth comes the moment to decide for the good or evil side. Woe to that man who in such a crisis chooses darkness rather than light! Better were it for that man that he had never been born. To-day the cause of evil may prosper, but Truth alone is strong, and around her "throng troops of beautiful, tall angels to enshield her from all wrong." To-day the swart kinsmen of Moses are slaves in the land of Goshen; to-morrow they are a royal priesthood, a nation of inspired prophets, disclosing the will of the Eternal One, and Moses is their anointed leader. There are two ways! Which will you choose? May that God who opened the eyes of Moses, and filled his heart with grace, humility, and wisdom, now grant unto you the power to choose the right, the brave, the true, and manly way! and may he uphold you therein until you and we and all of us ascend on high to swell the number of those who, having "gotten the victory over the beast, and over his image, and over his mark, and over the number of his name, stand on the sea of glass, mingled with fire, and sing the song of MOSES the servant of God, and the song of the Lamb, saying, Great and marvelous are thy works, Lord God Almighty; just and true are thy ways, thou King of saints!"

SIGNIFICANT OMISSIONS IN THE PREACHING OF JESUS.

From that time Jesus began to preach, and to say, Repent: for the kingdom of heaven is at hand.—Matt. iv, 17.

JESUS was a perpetual surprise to his contemporaries. He did and said many things for which they were totally unprepared, and he left undone and unsaid those things they confidently expected him to do and to say. The leaders of Jewish thought and politics at that time were sharply disappointed in him at every fresh phase of his life. They looked for the political restoration of Israel. He seemed almost utterly indifferent to their political condition and ambitions. They were hedging about the law with confusing and cumbersome traditions, making it hard for plain people to be good. He openly antagonized their exacting and oppressive ceremonial observances, and declared himself and his disciples forever free from the narrow and vain "traditions of men." They expected their Messiah to impose the Mosaic regulations upon the Gentile nations, or, in the event of their contumacy, to thresh them as with a rod of iron. He taught that all the law and the prophets consisted in loving God with the whole heart, and one's neighbor as one's self. They looked forward to a time when all nations should flow to

Jerusalem as the one acknowledged center of the world's political light and governance, as well as of its religious faith and worship. He taught a guilty and proscribed Samaritan woman that the time had come when honest, open-hearted men might every-where worship the Father in spirit and in truth. They demanded of him who should redeem Israel that he should maintain himself in gorgeous royal state, that he should surround himself with glittering earthly pomp and splendor, that his strong right arm should be swift to execute vengeance upon his foes, and that with swelling pride and power he should put his foot upon the neck of his prostrate enemies. He spent by far the greater portion of his life among rude and plain people, not differing in outward appearance, dress, and carriage markedly from his compatriots. He selected his inner circle of disciples from among the ranks of the common people; he daily lived with them on terms of equality and familiarity, and the occupation which wholly absorbed his time and energies was that of a simple and ardent preacher of obedience to God and love to man. Is it any wonder that his contemporaries should be keenly disappointed in him?

How does Jesus appear to modern thought? Is there not something strange and unexpected about him even to us? Remembering who he was, standing squarely upon our doctrinal basis, namely, that he was God manifest in the flesh, that the life he lived was the divine life, subject to physical and time conditions, was his course and manner of life such as we should have imagined beforehand? This is our faith, that in him dwelt all the fullness of the Godhead bodily, and holding fast by this, I ask, Did he live and act as we should have supposed God to live and act were he to appear in human form? Remember his great words to Philip, " He that hath seen me hath seen the Father." Does his life seem a natural one in the eyes of the modern man? Especially, so far forth as he was a preacher and teacher, was his preaching and teaching what we would have expected under the conditions supposed? Have you ever marked, and, marking, have you *observed, mused, reflected upon*, the singular and striking omissions of Jesus as a preacher? Do you ever reflect upon what he did *not* preach about? And have you reflected upon the significance of these omissions? For we may be sure that in his silence and reserve there is a revelation of God's will. Consider some of the subjects which, so far as we can observe or discover, never directly or formally entered into his preaching.

He does not anywhere discuss the subject of war; its horribleness, its cruelty, its futility as a means of settling disputes among nations, its sinfulness, or the best method of ridding the world of the awful curse. He, the Prince of Peace, never once, as far as we can find out, preached a sermon on war. He is likewise silent on the general subject of slavery, although the world was groaning under the gigantic wrong! He gave not a single hint, directly and avowedly, as to how men were to proceed in order to secure universal emancipation. At no time or place did he take up and consider the vitally important question of the relation of woman to the State, to the government, to education, to man, to the general welfare. It is a modern unbeliever who writes of the alleged "subjugation of woman." It is in vain that we search the reported discourses of Jesus to ascertain his mind as to the best form of government among men—a subject of vast importance, and concerning which good and wise men widely differ. There is not a single paragraph in any of his sermons as to the relative importance of the physical, mental, and moral elements of human evolution and civilization. He is utterly silent as to the influence of art on civilization, on religion, on liberty, on general progress. He sketched no plan, gave us the outline of no scheme, for the reorganization of society.

He did not anticipate any of the methods of modern philosophy or study, or any of the great discoveries of modern science, or their application to the conduct and comforts of life.

What, then, I am asked, did he preach about? The text tells us—"Repent." This was the heart and substance of his preaching. Comprehensively this sums it all up, compacts it for us. We must not forget what this word "Repent" contains or includes in the preaching of Jesus. It includes every active process by which men break with evil, its seduction and thrall; all that we mean by conviction, penitence, abandonment of evil, faith, consecration, prayer, and the like. It meant an immediate, radical, profound *change and evolution* in a man's moral life. It included all that was necessary, on man's part, to enable him to become in very deed a partaker of the Divine Nature, a sharer of God's holiness.

What may we learn from this opening up of the passage?

1. In the estimate of the divine Jesus, sin is not only a real and stubborn fact, but an awful, ruinous, and tremendous fact. What does he do? He comes, a God, to redeem the world, and where and how does he begin? With the customs of men, their conditions, or laws, or institutions? On the outside? Nay, but at the very center of personal, individual moral being. What is his evident, chief, glowing concern for men? Is it not that they shall be at once rescued from the thrall and service of evil? We may be sure that he, God manifest in the flesh, would give himself at once to the detection, the uprooting, the extirpation of that form of danger and peril which he believed most seriously menaced man's true life; and, judging by his deeds, his works, his disposition, and his words, that peril was the dread and awful mystery we seek to express by the word "sin."

See the wide difference at this point between Jesus, and the thought and conduct of men. Men even dispute the reality of sin as a fact, and allege that if it is a fact it is a light, easy, trivial, venial matter. If men do not, in so many words, *say* these things, they act as if these things were true. Judging men by their lives, by their deeds, by their daily conduct, what do they say? They confess that certain things are to be dreaded—as pain, ignorance, poverty, labor, disease, death. By their acts are they not saying that poverty is more to be dreaded than evil, pain than sin, toil than covetousness? Are not most men seeking, first, in point of time, of importance, of earnestness, health, knowledge, longevity, comfort, place, position, power, wealth, luxury? What, after all, is the strenuous endeavor of human life as we see it about us? Is it righteousness? Is it God's peace? Or, is it wealth, power, fame?

Let us remember, then, what is hidden in any fair, straightforward, honest interpretation of these words of the Lord Jesus; namely, that sin is the sternest and awfulest fact with which we have to do, that moral evil is the evil most to be dreaded and fought.

2. In the divine thought and purpose, as disclosed to us in the life and preaching of Jesus, the redemption of man from the evils which afflict, oppress, and weaken him is to be effected, not all at once, by direct divine fiat or sovereign decree, but slowly and gradually, through the regeneration of the individual, man by man, one at a time. I have said that Jesus omitted war, slavery, woman, government, education, art, as formal topics in his preaching. But was he indifferent to war? Did he have no sympathy with the slaves? Recked he not as to whether men lived under tyrants or

exulted in liberty? We may not suppose for a single moment that Jesus was not concerned as to these matters. By all his love for us, these things must have deeply concerned him. We know in fact that they did. He must have designed their overthrow and destruction, so far as they annoy, and vex, and enthrall, and weaken, and destroy us. How does he mean to effect it? By first making each man right, pure, and sound, beginning with repentance. The answer is in the text: "Repent." This word comes to each man, in his own sole, direct, immediate responsibility, and not to men in groups. The word is not to men in states and nations, "Repent, change your laws, customs, policies, institutions, etc.," but to each individual man the word is, "Repent, change your own heart and life, turn from evil, lay hold on all that is good." This is the plan of Jesus.

There is another method; that, namely, of the world. It proposes the removal of evils, the relief of man's distresses by giving him perfect conditions. By understanding it, we will be enabled to gain an insight into the weakness of the method of the average professional social and legislative reformer. What does this method say? As to war, for example: "Form peace societies, substitute arbitration for the sword, appeal to the self-interest of the people, disarm the nations." This would all do very well if it took the war-spirit—the spirit that foments and breeds war—out of men's hearts. "Change your laws, your customs, your institutions, and this evil will disappear," is the message of the average professional reformer.

Contrast with this the slower, the more patient, less showy, more thorough-going method of Jesus. His message is, "Change your men, and evils of all kinds will gradually and surely disappear." Test his method. Consider, for example, this vexatious tenement-house question. Of what use are your laws against the grasping landlord, or any other social criminal, unless you change him in nature, heart, disposition? He will only change his form of oppression and cruelty, just as fast as you change your laws, unless by repentance, faith, prayer, you take the greed and selfishness out of him. It is precisely so with the temperance reform. The average professional temperance reformer says, "Take liquor away from men, and intemperance will cease." Certainly, but for how long a time? Until the man can get to it again. Jesus says, "Make men stronger than liquor; by repentance, faith, conversion, take the bad appetite out of men, utterly uproot it, change their hearts, and liquor will disappear."

Did we not find at the close of the war, in the case of the negroes, that emancipation did not mean character. Were we not compelled to take them, man by man, and gradually restore, recover, and regenerate them, one at a time? Did we not recognize this, and at once begin the work? And are we not at it now, with our societies, schools, and churches?

The Christianity of Jesus is the sole hope of the world. Every time we adopt the methods of shallow social empirics, we weaken our cause and postpone the day of the world's salvation. It is slow, but it recognizes the stern fact of SIN. Its message is still what it was at the first, "Repent." There is indeed to be a perfect society in this world, but it will be composed of perfect men. Brethren, another world is to come, and we, according to his promise, look for a new heaven and a new earth, wherein dwelleth righteousness. The perfect world of which we dream is coming, but it will be here only when this world is filled with perfect men; when each man in the world hears and obeys for himself the divine command, "Repent;" when each man breaks with the evil that enthralls him, casts out of him every thing that defileth, and sets up within his own heart that love, and righteousness, and joy in which is the kingdom of God. May that blessed day hasten!

3. Our discernment of the reality and nearness of the kingdom of heaven is conditioned upon the genuineness and thoroughness of our repentance. Is there a kingdom of heaven at all? Is it not all a dream? Has God a kingdom here? Men ominously shake their heads, and say, "No; there may be a kingdom of heaven, but it is not here. Where are the signs of it? The Lord is slack concerning his promise." The words they speak and the adverse signs to which they point cannot dim our faith. "Alas!" they say, "our hearts are sick

through deferred hope. If there be a kingdom of heaven at all, one thing is quite certain—it is not here. There may be one somewhere else; perhaps there is, we hope there is; but there is none here in this world."

Jesus speaks directly to the contrary. He says it *is here;* it " is *at hand.*" My business is to explain and vindicate his words. It is " at hand." This he says every-where and always, quietly and calmly.

Here again is obvious discrepancy, direct, sharp collision, between what men see and say, and what Jesus saw and said. How is it to be explained? The single word "Repent" explains it, but we must remember how much he makes that word to mean. We will not see that kingdom except we repent. He never promised that we should see it on any other condition. It is given to the heavenly minded man to see the kingdom of heaven, to the godlike man to see the kingdom of God, just as it is given to the noble-minded man to see nobleness, and the pure-minded man to see purity.

Have you not, at blessed and glorious intervals, caught a glimpse of the kingdom of heaven? Did you not on some bright day, some day of straight thinking and clear seeing, some day when you were caught up and beheld things which it is impossible for a man to utter, begin to discern the outlines of a divine order and rule in this world? When, how, under what conditions, did it please God to vouchsafe you the vision? It was when you felt yourself to be in blessed sympathy with God. Into this kingdom we will enter and abide, if our repentance be genuine, thorough, lasting.

The preaching of Jesus brings a universal message of mercy, love, and hope. To whom does this word come? To a select and favored class? No, but to all men. Mark well the form of the words, "Repent ye," not, "Be ye repented." Is not this message one of large mercy and hope?

See yonder man, the victim of a hideous disorder. He is broken out all over with loathsome ulcers, repulsive to his friends, a burden and a misery to himself, his life surely slipping away. The quack's prescription is, "Cover the ulcers with flesh-like plasters, and you will surely grow better." Is this merciful treatment? Is there any hope in it? And what now does his intelligent and kind physician say? "Repent; repent at once; change *immediately* your whole manner of life. The change must be instant, radical, thorough. It must include your food, and drink, and associations, and sleep, and air, every thing. Do this, and the kingdom of health is at hand. Your ulcers will disappear, and you will be once more a well and strong man." Is not this the message the man needs, and is it not full of mercy and hope? This is the message of Jesus to men. Yes, it is his message this day to you. In imitation of him, I declare to you, in his name and on his gracious authority, "Repent! Repent! the kingdom of heaven is at hand." Enter it. Keep its laws. Give it the first place in your plan of life. If you will submit yourself to the rule and service of its King he will guide you by his counsels here, and afterward he will receive you to glory!

THE MORAL HARVEST.

Say not ye, There are yet four months, and then cometh harvest? behold, I say unto you, Lift up your eyes, and look on the fields; for they are white already to harvest.—John iv, 35.

JESUS was a most unconventional teacher. Looked at from one side—from the point of view occupied by the pious, steady-going, orthodox Jews—he was an irregular and disturbing preacher, and they so esteemed him. Looked at in a larger and broader spirit, and from a higher stand-point, as the divine Founder of an enduring, invisible, spiritual empire, uncaring of the accidents of race and time and clime and caste, his course was eminently rational, natural, and inevitable.

The immediate context brings Jesus before us, where we may study him as an irregular Teacher if we take the narrow view; or as an eminently regular Teacher if we take the truer, broader, and more sympathetic view.

As he was returning from the city of Jerusalem to Galilee, after his first formal official visit to the capital of his nation, he reached, about noon, Jacob's well in Samaria, and there, wearied and over-spent, he sat down upon the stones hard by the well, while his disciples went into the city to buy some meat. What were his communings and thoughts as he sat there? Nothing is more impressive than the silences of Jesus. I love to think of him as alone; and it is a help to one's spiritual life to try to imagine what he thought about at such times.

While he was musing there and resting—for he was a man having a body capable of fatigue as our bodies—a woman of the city came with her waterpot on her head or shoulder to get water from Jacob's well. He knew who and what manner of woman she was before he spoke one word to her. Her heart and her life lay open before him like the pages of a book. Nevertheless he freely entered into conversation with her, and his method of approaching her with the truth deserves to be noted, studied, and emphasized. First, he asked her for water to drink, and she was surprised that he, being a Jew, should ask drink of a woman of Samaria, for the Jews had no dealings with the Gentiles, and she at once expressed her great surprise. Whereupon Jesus replied that if she knew what kind of water he could give to her spirit she would ask him, and he would give her this living water. Thereupon she reproached him for believing himself to be wiser and stronger than their father Jacob, who gave them this well; and upon Jesus telling her that whosoever drank of the water of the well should thirst again, but that they who should have their spirits satisfied by the living water should never thirst, she at once wanted this living water, for she did not want to be constantly going to this well to draw water.

There are a good many people like her in this respect. There are many people who want water, but they do not want to draw it. She was not the only lazy person that ever lived. And if you spiritualize it, there are a great many people that want religious strength and peace, and religious joy and hope, but they do not want to draw any water; they do not want to do any Christian work; they do not want to make any sacrifice, or to deny themselves, that they may have Christ's peace.

Then Jesus said unto her, "Go and call thy husband." Ah! that opened a door into her secret heart, for she had no husband. She had had five husbands, and the man with whom she was now living was her paramour, and not her husband. At once she felt herself in the presence of a divinely gifted teacher. And how did she seek to parry the inquiry? By raising a question in theology— "Where is it right to worship—on this mountain, or yonder at Jerusalem?" Guilty as she was, she could still argue points in speculative theology, and so she wanted to know whether it was better to worship on Gerizim or go up to Jerusalem. The Lord answered her that the time had come when sincere men might worship the Father in spirit and in truth anywhere, every-where, either on Gerizim or at Jerusalem, or at any point between them, on the land or the sea, in the consecrated building, or on the unconsecrated street—wherever there was a spirit that loved truth and sought goodness.

While he was talking with the woman his disciples came back from the city, where they had been to buy meat for the frugal noon-day meal. They were surprised when they saw him talking to her; the text says " they marveled." If you will study the New Testament you will be surprised at the anxious concern these disciples had about the proper conduct of Jesus. They are like a certain class of people in every church, who are so anxious about the preacher, and about his reputation, that it shall be kept regular, clean, and decorous, that they almost forget to take care of their own souls. These disciples were anxious their Lord should not do any thing irregular, so when they saw him talking to this strange woman they " marveled." But they did not care to ask him any thing about it. Jesus was the ideal, social Democrat of all time—he talked freely to all sorts of people. But he never allowed any body to ask him why he did it. He had true dignity, the dignity of person, of soul, of character, and these men who were surprised that he talked to this heretical woman (who added to laxity of doctrine looseness of life), these men whispered among themselves, but they did not dare to ask him why he talked to her.

It seemed to them that the Master was in a dreamy, far-off sort of mood. They began to talk to him about eating, and he said, " I have meat to eat that ye know not of." They entirely misunderstood him again, for they went aside and asked, " Has any man brought him to eat?" His mind and spirit were in another realm; they were thinking about the meat they had with them.

The barley fields that covered the valley all about prophesied harvest in four months, and, waiting for him to speak (for they had learned somewhat to respect the personal dignity of their Master), they were saying to themselves, " In four months from this time it will be time to cut the barley;" and he said, "Say not ye, There are yet four months, and then cometh harvest? behold, I say unto you, Lift up your eyes, and look on the fields; for they are white already to harvest." They saw the barley fields; and he saw the harvest field that was opened before him by the presence and life of this woman. He was thinking of far more than they thought, as he had a yearning for men far deeper than any they had. He saw the moral harvest ready for the sickle of the reaper every-where; but their minds were busy about the barley harvest.

There be those who are skilled to discern times and seasons and opportune tides in the affairs of men in every realm except the spiritual and invisible. These disciples, for example, knew the time to cut barley; the Jewish leaders of this time could seize a political opportunity; they knew exactly how to strike a bargain with Herod—they had studied Herod, and rightly estimated the influences that put him in his place; they understood Pilate, and when the time came to apprehend the Master they knew exactly what cry would bring Pilate to terms; they understood facts and times and seasons and opportunities like these. But they did not discern the real signs of the times, and our Lord again and again reproached them for their ignorance in true moral discernment.

There are men who can tell all about times and seasons in the social, political, and commercial worlds. There are farmers who know when it is time to sow and to reap; there are merchants who know when to buy and when to sell; there are those who know when to buy real estate; there are a good many men who know when to buy real estate at the lowest, and they would seem to have an almost divinely gifted capacity of knowing when to sell it at the highest. I have in mind a preacher (it was no fault of his) who made money by buying and selling real estate. The truth of it was that he was originally intended to be a money-maker, and he could not help buying property when it was low and selling it when it was high. There are men who know when to buy "long" and when to buy "short" in the market. There are men who know what the political drifts are. The popular voice is so strong in these days that no politician any more pretends to tell the people what they ought to do. The science of politics is reduced to finding out what the people are going to have done, and then making haste to get on that side of the fence. There are many men skilled to discern the force and direction of political drifts and currents.

But when, in the realm of moral activity, there

be those who maintain that there are times and seasons, that there is a time to sow and a time to reap; that there are times for ingatherings and times for aggression, there be some who say, " O no, not in religion; in religion all goes along regularly; in religion every thing must be smooth; in religion there is to be no sudden influx of people; in religion there must be no waves of excitement, no seasons of great interest; in religion all must be quiet and orderly." The result of which is that churches are now waiting in some mysterious way for God to go to these people that are without hope and without righteousness and without love, and compel them to embrace the religious life. There *are* times and seasons in religion; there *are* times when the harvests are ripe. You may be surprised at the statement, you may be disposed to resent it, but there are preachers who know more about signs and indications in the moral realm than any other man in the Church. I assert for the ministers of Christ, where they are sincere and earnest, a superior capacity to detect and discern such drifts, such tendencies, such signs. I would be regarded as an impertinent meddler should I go into the counting-room of any man in this church and tell him when to buy and sell. He would justly tell me that he had mastered his business, that he had been apprenticed to it for years, and understood its secrets and knew when to buy and sell. And so I affirm that where a preacher's heart is wholly in this matter, where he gives himself to the service of religion with hearty and entire devotion, the judgment of the average faithful pastor concerning the spiritual phenomena is truer than that of any other man in the community. Jesus knew better than the disciples, better than the world, when the harvest was ripe; and so if one will devote his life to the study of spiritual phenomena he can foretell spiritual results with surprising prescience.

I remark again, that we should closely inquire into the causes of that weakness of spiritual vision by which we either dimly see, or do not see at all, the whiteness of religious harvest fields. It was important, indeed, that these disciples should know why it was that Jesus saw what they did not see. They saw barley fields; he saw the field of the world. They had meat in their baskets, and he saw the hunger of the human spirit. There was some ground for the difference between them—what was it? Was the fault in the moral opaqueness of the disciples, or in the fact that after all there was no harvest field ready for the sickle? Jesus saw a harvest field; they did not see it. Why did not they see it?

The first reason was that they were narrow and bigoted. "The Jews have no dealing with the Samaritans." If Jesus had not been with them, and they had reached the well, and this woman of Samaria had come where they were, they would have gathered up their holy skirts and moved off as though she was a foul and accursed thing; they would have had nothing to do with her. They were more anxious about food for their bodies than food for such souls.

Nor is this all. They were proud. This woman—who is she? This woman that has had five husbands, and is now living in a loose way with a man who is not her husband—shall we speak to her, or tarry with her? Certainly not! That was their spirit.

Not only so, but it was a spirit of selfishness. They thought: "We have the Master to ourselves, and we will keep him; John shall be secretary of state, James shall be secretary of war, and Peter shall be prime minister of the new kingdom. Do you suppose we will share the Messiah with this low woman?" They had the spirit of monopoly, the spirit of accursed caste, the most devilish spirit that ever escaped from the nether kingdom. No wonder men possessed of such a spirit could see no fields ready for the harvest.

Friends, weakness of vision does not always argue that there is nothing to see. Weakness of vision may argue the decaying power of the orb of vision. I go to a saloon, I go to a race-course, I go to some gambling hell, and I take a man that lives in his eyes and ears, and especially in his mouth and stomach. He has been living there for many years; food and drink, and every thing that pampers and gratifies his body, have made up his life. I say to him, "Come with me, and I will show you the higher joys and deeper pleasures of the intellect, the heart, the conscience," and I take him to the schools, or the home circle, or to the church, where people live in a higher realm of being; where they live in books, in ideas, in pictures, and in music; where they live in the holy loves of the family, of purity, of righteousness, live unselfishly, self sacrificingly—and I say to him, "Look at these things." And he says, "I don't see any thing so very attractive about all this. I call it stale, flat, insipid. Do you ever go to a race? Did you ever hear the glasses clink in the bar-room? Did you ever drink to a man's health? That is poor stuff there—looking at pictures, singing hymns, and reading books." To him it is tame and flat. Why? Because there are no pure pleasures here? No; but because he has no eyes to see. And why is it that so many do not see the harvest fields in the world? Because they have no eyes to see guilt and moral misery; because they have nothing that enables them to touch with the skillful tact of love the guilty, frail, and breaking hearts that long have waited for the light and love of God!

The spirit of Jesus, by which he was enabled to see these harvest fields, is to be had only by those who obey his laws and enter into his spirit. Now let us take this scene and break it up into its parts, in order that we may learn why Jesus saw what the disciples did not see. The first thing he saw was that here was an opportunity to preach the Gospel to one woman. Well, many preachers of the present time would not have accepted the opportunity. The disciples would not have accepted it. That was a strange pulpit — the stones of Jacob's well — and what an unusual audience it was: one person, and she a woman! To be a woman even now implies some disadvantages ; but *then* to be a woman was to be— a good deal less than a man! This was an heretical woman; this was an immoral woman; and yet, standing on the stones of Jacob's well, with one auditor, and she a heretic, Jesus preached one of the greatest sermons he ever preached, and announced some of the most wonderful of his teachings. We would not have done it, many of us ; we would have waited for a larger and a more respectable audience ; we would have waited to preach such a sermon in some great place; but Jesus had in him the spirit that never despised any opportunity to preach or to do good.

In the next place, he had the secret of reverent courage. I do not mean the courage that is confounded with audacity or recklessness. I mean reverent courage, courage that could fearlessly face and sternly rebuke the traditional spirit that remorselesly crushed human hearts. He would not take away one jot or tittle of the law, but all the traditions that men had invented and tacked on to the law—he denounced them, and broke away from them, as here. He talked to a woman to whom no Jewish priest would have dared to have said a word.

He had the spirit of sympathy; a gift, I sometimes fear, which is rapidly dying out of the Church. He knew the ache at this woman's heart, and there are few people any more who even pretend to know it. He knew the visions that came to her of her lost innocence and purity; he knew that she thought of the time when she was a girl as pure as the flowers that grew by the side of the paths along which she walked, or as pure as the heaven into which she looked. There are those who seem to deny that there are any aches in the hearts of those who are far from goodness and purity. Sunday after Sunday, men and women enter the doors of our churches and from their faces or words you would not know the heavy burdens they carry; and how few there be who know that these souls need help and kindness and sympathy!

The spirit of Jesus, once more, was the spirit of open communion with the Father! "I have meat to eat that ye know not of." He was thinking of food for his spirit, they of food for their bodies; he was thinking of his Father, "I must finish the work my Father sent me to do;" and they were thinking how long it would be until the reapers would cut down the barley. So it was that Jesus, living in open communion with his Father, saw what was hidden from his disciples.

Whoever will take life's humblest opportunities and be faithful to them, whoever will have reverent courage, the courage that takes off the hat before qualities and keeps it on in the presence of mere semblances, a courage that could strike down tradition and lift up a guilty woman, the spirit that could question tradition and die for purity—

whoever has this spirit, and the spirit of open communion with God, will see the white harvest fields of the world. Lift up your eyes and look upon them! Lift up your eyes and look upon the fields covered by the words *honest doubt*. Do you know that there is such a thing as honest doubt? Do you know that there are a great many aching hearts now in the condition of honest doubters? You think not. When an aged woman tells me, as she washes and irons in the fourth story of a tenement house, in a small room as hot as a furnace, that her son-in-law has amassed a large fortune, and is a member of a great church, and her daughter has thousands at her disposal, I can know something about why she should ask, " Where is He whom I have served from my earliest childhood?" That is not a question that infidels ask; that is a question forced out of a suffering human heart by the hardness of life's lot. She is not alone in such questionings.

Lift up your eyes and look upon the fields that are indicated by the words *pain* and *suffering*. Have you any idea how much pain and suffering there is in the world that needs the message of the Gospel? Have you ever, when your nerves throbbed with pain, have you ever, when your system was in a fierce fire of fever, have you ever thought then, not of your own present personal suffering, but of the great world's agony? Do you know anything of what the great Garfield once called "the undiscovered mystery of pain?" and do you have any pity at all for those who live lives of pain and suffering?

Lift up your eyes and look upon the field represented by guilt, by moral waste, wretchedness, and misery. Do you ever think of that field? How many young men are there, do you suppose, in New York and Brooklyn, who are being wasted and will be ruined before the middle of next April? Not less than ten thousand! A close observer estimates that New York and Brooklyn, with the out-lying towns, constitute the moral maelstrom which swallows up ten thousand unwary youths every year. Dead from rum, dead from lust, dead from gambling, dead by the pistol, dead by the plunge into the dark river! Do you see them? Do you see the fields that are white already unto the harvest? Do you still ask me to be calm, do you still ask me to be decorous and quiet, do you still ask me to be content with the moral indifference I see about me? I might if I did not partially see the field; but He who sat, weary, on the stones of Jacob's well has so far led me into his spirit that I see somewhat of the need of the world—the hunger of man's spirit for God, the yearning of the human heart for the divine love. I seem to see the feet that are slipping, slipping, slipping! I seem to hear the voices of those that cry out, "No man careth for my soul!" I seem to see and to be touched with a feeling of sympathy for those whose hearts ache over a lost purity!

O that God would give so much of his Spirit to all his Churches, and so spur them to prayer, and faith, and work, and love, that if a woman of

Samaria should come down the broad aisle of our most wealthy and aristocratic church all hearts would be melted at the sight of the woman's penitence! And then, after a hundred years, would that God might raise up a Church divine enough, and Christ-like enough, not to wait until such came down the aisle, but would seek them out, and bring them to the healing and benignant Christ! O that we all might henceforth enter into the "unhasting, unresting" activity of Jesus, in which is the peace and blessedness and power of God!

THE GREATNESS OF JESUS.

And the Jews marveled, saying, How knoweth this man 'etters, having never learned? Jesus answered them, and said, My doctrine is not mine, but his that sent me. If any man will do his will, he shall know of the doctrine, whether it be of God, or whether I speak of myself.—John vii, 15-17.

For such a high-priest became us, who is holy, harmless, undefiled, separate from sinners, and made higher than the heavens.— Heb. vii, 26.

THE intellectual doubter of the nineteenth century is accustomed to speak of Jesus in terms of high laudation. He extols his singular purity of character, his gentleness and graciousness of demeanor, his kindness and patience and forbearance to those who opposed themselves, his tender sympathy with the poor, the weak, the wronged, and the suffering, his devoted, disinterested life, and the meekness and mercifulness of the spirit in which he met his death. He is spoken of as "the greatest Hebrew," yea, as "the greatest man" who has ever appeared in the entire history of the world; he was a great reformer, a great religious teacher, a profound moral philosopher. The human race is vastly, yea, immeasurably, indebted to him; he has inspired and stimulated and directed the progress, the moral progress especially, of mankind, as no other character known to us; his contributions to human virtue, and hence to human happiness, have been greater than those of any other single member of the race. These are the expressions frequently found on the lips of those who preserve either a neutral or a hostile attitude to the divine claims of Jesus Christ. Our Lord was once buried in a rock-tomb; he is in danger now of being buried in a grave of flowers — beautiful and fragrant flowers they are, but they have been secretly sprinkled with concealed deadly poison. We who own him as the Master of our souls, as the supreme Lord of our worship, and love, and duty, and life, are not thus tamely to surrender him to his foes. He is more than a great Hebrew, more than an inspired prophet, more than an acute and eminent religious reformer, more than a profound moral philosopher, more than a highly gifted moral genius—" He is over all, God blessed for evermore!"

In seeking to-night to ascertain who and what he was, in a calm and reverent and earnest way, I assume the fewest possible number of universally conceded facts. I assume that there was born in Palestine, nearly nineteen hundred years ago, the person we call Jesus; that his reputed parents were plain, ordinary, humble Jewish folk, without either genius or rank or wealth; that he spent his youth and grew to manhood in the contemned and degraded province of Galilee; that at the age of thirty or thereabout he publicly assumed the functions of a religious teacher; that four short sketches of his life were written either by men who companied with him from the beginning or who had access to original sources of information; that these sketches contain a reliable account of what he said, of how he lived, of the substance of his teaching, of what manner of man he was; that the leaders of the Jewish people believed him to be a disturbing, dangerous, and revolutionary teacher, and that, prompted by the mixed motives of religious zeal, selfishness, and envy, they brought about his death under the procuratorship of Pontius Pilate; and that the Christian religion, with all that these great words imply, sprang from what he said and did and was. I do not, for the purposes of this hour, take for granted the reality of any of the supernatural works that the writers of these lives ascribe to him. I simply assume that he appeared, acted, and taught in substance as these lives record; and on this strong basis of solid fact, now conceded by all competent scholars and thinkers, I ask you candidly and dispassionately to study with me his intellectual and moral greatness, and see if they do not significantly point with great, ever-increasing, and at last convincing force to his superhumanity in nature and origin.

The intellectual greatness of Jesus will appear if we consider his entire independence of circumstances. Intellectual greatness is not an uncaused phenomenon. To beings like ourselves, with our faculties and range of vision, whatever *is* must come from something that has been. We are not living in a blind, an orderless, a causeless universe. It is the latest dictum of science itself that for every phenomenon there must be some adequate explanaation—not only that every effect must have a cause, but that every effect must have a rational and competent cause. Intellectual facts or phenomena do not constitute an exception to this general rule. They, too, are in the vise of law. Intellectual power has its conditions, its necessary antecedents. You are aware that a certain class of scholars have been somewhat puzzled concerning the intellectual greatness of Shakespeare, for there is exhibited in his tragedies and comedies and historical dramas not only marvelous mental acuteness and fertility, not only an accurate and profound knowledge of human nature, but no inconsiderable amount of what we technically style learning. How, now, did he obtain this knowledge? The earlier part of Shakespeare's life is wrapped in comparative obscurity; our information concerning that period is not as ample as could be desired, and those who are dissatisfied with the theory of the Shakesperean authorship of the works usually attributed to him assign as the reason for their objection that no explanation can be given of his remarkable historical knowledge, or any time specified when he could have acquired the large general information unquestionably exhibited in his dramas and tragedies. Lord Bacon had the time and the opportunities necessary to acquire this information, and he is the only contemporary of Shakespeare who seems to have possessed the needed original intellectual qualifications; and the hypothesis of this class of reasoners is that Bacon is the author of the so-called Shakesperean plays.

The question is precisely what it was with the Jews in our Lord's day. " How knoweth this man letters, having never learned?" Mark well the circumstances of Jesus, how confining and dulling and deadening they were. There was nothing in his immediate family to predict intellectual greatness; there was nothing in his early occupation that would naturally lead to intellectual greatness; his native country was not an intellectual country, such as Greece; he never attended any famous school; he never traveled outside of Palestine, and therefore he could not know the broadening, liberalizing, educating effects of foreign travel; whatever scholastic training he received must have been in the school connected with the synagogue, in the village of Nazareth. We are sufficiently familiar with the general spirit of these schools, and of the eminent teachers of his time, to know that, so far from such instruction having a tendency to lead forth and strengthen the intellectual faculties, the contrary was the truth : that these schools and teachers were occupied with small and petty questions of days, washings, tithes, slavish traditions, and various oppressive legalisms, and that they omitted the weightier matters of the law, such as justice and judgment, morality and truth. Such were the surroundings of Jesus, and yet it is freely confessed by all men that he rose superior to the dwarfing and deadening power of these circumstances; that alike in his personal spirit and in the scope and substance of his teaching he was unlike any rabbi who might have taught him; utterly unlike his countrymen; that he was conspicuously free from any of the influences that must have gathered about him during his boyhood and youth in the province of Galilee.

Not only so, but he showed himself to be absolutely above the power of circumstances. He exhibited that high and peculiar kind of intellectual greatness which shows its presence and power by the removal of obstacles, by the mastery of circumstances, by the conquest of difficulties. One who has had such intellectual opportunities as were afforded the late Mr. Sumner is expected to achieve intellectual eminence; and the reason why, in the future history of this country, it will be confessed that Abraham Lincoln was a greater man than Mr. Sumner is that with no such opportunities as the Massachusetts senator, either in the public school, or the academy, or the university, or by foreign travel, or by association with the scholarly and the cultured, he was found, when called to a perilous post in a great national crisis, to be greater with slight opportunities than Mr. Sumner with ample and splendid opportunities. It is the presence in Jesus of this form of intellectual greatness, to a degree absolutely unique and unparalleled, which more and more attracts the attention of thoughtful men in their study of the vast influence which he has hitherto exercised, and which he seems to continue to exercise, on the thought and conduct of the best and strongest men of the race.

In the second place, Jesus pierced at once to the

heart of things, and saw the truth as in open vision. There are two ways of arriving at truth—by logic and by insight: by reasoning to it, and by divining it; by laboriously plodding after it, and by simply finding it. The latter is one of the great characteristics of genius. The presence of fruitful genius in any great department of human thought or activity is betokened by the power to see at a glance what other men, tardy-footed, reach by slow and laborious processes. Jesus SAW the truth. He seldom argued about it; he seldom reasoned about it. There is no formal argument for the existence of God, for the obligatoriness of duty, for the spiritual nature and destiny of man in the preserved discourses of Jesus. He was open to the truth, and the truth was open to him. He found it by seeing it; he simply announced, declared, uttered what he saw, and there is not a single hint or suggestion anywhere that he came to his truth by any dialectical method. The relation of logic to the truth of Jesus is the same as that of the technique of music to the singing of the meadow lark on a May morning. To the religious mind there is much truth in the parable of the prodigal son—more truth than many of us have capacity as yet to receive. But there is no major premiss in it, there is no minor premiss, there is no formal drawing of a conclusion from foregoing premisses, no acute dialectics. It is a picture: a picture of what the heart of a truly loving father is toward a wayward, guilty, and repentant son, and as painted by Jesus it is a picture of what the heart of God perpetually is to all his wayward children. But he did not argue it; he did not prove it; he SAW it as in open vision, and then painted the picture in a few simple words.

The quality of the truth thus disclosed by Jesus needs to be briefly emphasized in passing. I take two examples of the peculiar and lofty quality of the truth which Jesus saw and declared: and, first, Jesus taught that the reformation of society is always to proceed by the divine regeneration of the individual. He never, indeed, stated it in that precise language. I cannot see things as he did; I must state them the best I can. Nevertheless, a patient study of the New Testament without bias and without prejudice impresses every thoughtful and reverent man with this truth, that Jesus aimed at the reformation of society by the regeneration of the individual. I mean, for example, that he did not aim at the reformation of society by the sudden or radical change of any institution. The cruel institution of slavery was cramping men then; the social state of woman was demoralizing in the extreme; he never formally considered these important topics. The civil laws that were then imposed upon the conquered nations by the Romans were crude, partial, at times sanguinary, but he made no proclamation for a reformation of the laws. He did teach, quietly, constantly, solemnly, that each individual man, by the pressure upon his heart and conscience of the truth, and by the efficient co-operation of a spiritual Power outside of man, should be re-molded and re-fashioned until the law of duty, as interpreted in the atmosphere of love, should be the law of his life. As you improve men themselves, they will gradually and permanently change their institutions. It requires no argument to see that if you make right men they will fashion for themselves right institutions. The world's way is to get right institutions, right laws, right customs, right methods and instruments, hoping that with these right men will appear. The method of Jesus was first to get right men, and then through them a right society, and so at last a right world would come. We are still very much in doubt about it, but whenever the world has won any new ground, and kept it, the secret of the permanent advance is to be found in the appearance of men and women who confess the presence in their hearts of the regenerating Spirit.

Another illustration of the quality of his truth may be stated in this language: Jesus declared that love was the supreme purifying agent in the soul of man. He did not teach that love was *a* purifying agent he did not teach that love was a *powerful* purifying agent, but he taught, with all possible clearness and emphasis, that love was the supreme, all-powerful, purifying agent in the spirit of man. The question how man's spirit is to be emancipated from the thrall and corruption of evil passions has ever been an earnest question with those who have been given to ethical thought. The Lord answered the question again and again by declaring, "Thou shalt love the Lord thy God with all thy heart, and mind, and soul, and strength, and thy neighbor as thyself." He never altered his teaching, never diminished it, never minified it, never compromised it, but to the very last he taught that the complete moral restoration and health of any human spirit was to proceed under the inspiring and cleansing mastery of love, and that for love there was no substitute in the heavens above or in the earth beneath. We are afraid to believe that; modern society does not even profess to believe it, and the Church, which does not profess to believe it, is busily engaged in paring it down, and trying to accommodate it to human infirmity and prejudice. I raise this question: How would you, how would society, how would the world, restore to purity a woman lost to it? The first answer to that question by the men of the world is that no actual reformation is possible. I speak advisedly: it is the deliberate opinion of a majority of the men of the world that such a woman is incapable of moral restoration. What we call "society," that is, "society" in Christian countries, practically declares that such a creature must be left to perish in her pollution. There is no possible cure for the evil; but by building up high walls, and walls as thick as high, society may so stigmatize the transgressor as to leave her in the outer darkness, without hope of purity and peace. The man who compassed the ruin may indeed be there received, may indeed be there honored, and feted, and flattered, but for the unhappy victim of his hellish lust society has no open door. The man of penalties, whether he be a natural scientist, or an austere agnostic, or a theologian of the letter, declares that the only reformation possible in such a case is by a strict infliction of the law of penalty. "She has sinned; she must now suffer the inevitable penalties of her sin. Show her to what an awful end she hastens; deter her by these terrors, and if they will not alarm her, nothing remains but the leap into the sullen river at night, to be followed by the unknown body awaiting identification at the morgue. Show her that not only in this life, but also in the life to come, the law of penalty shall pursue and smite and destroy." Now, suppose there could be born in such a creature (I do not say that such a thing is possible, but we will try to imagine it), suppose there was born in her heart a holy love—I care not whether it be for man or woman, so that in her deepest spiritual nature a genuine overmastering affection for some pure soul is born—is there not hope? And is there any other hope? There was such a woman once in a Galilean town, and at a feast where the rich and the powerful and the learned were, came the sinful and the fair, and the giver of the feast sneered and scorned, and the disciples gathered close about the Lord, fearful lest he might be compromised as she stooped and bowed her head, and rained her hot tears down on his unsandaled feet, and loosed the long tresses of her hair, that she might wipe away the signs of her shame and penitence. And what did he say? "Her sins, which are many, are forgiven, for she loved much." For she loved much! In the teaching of Jesus, *love* is the prophecy of coming purity, light, and peace!

These two truths are universal; they will always apply; they will apply under a government by aristocracy, under a government by monarchy, under a government by democracy; they will apply in the frigid zone, where it is difficult to baptize people by immersion, and they will apply also in the torrid zone, where immersion is the natural mode of baptism; they will apply where the genius of the people would lead them to reject Calvinism, and they will apply where the genius of the people would lead them to reject Arminianism. These two fundamental truths of Jesus—that the reformation of society is to proceed by the regeneration of the individual, and that in the restoration of a guilty soul nothing whitens like the glowing fires of love— apply every-where, apply in all places and under all circumstances, apply under every condition known to man. We need to fix it in our hearts that for this race on this globe there will never come a time when they will be outworn or fall into desuetude. They are more real and abiding than the solid bases of the everlasting mountains. The Eternal is in them.

The intellectual greatness of Jesus will appear if we consider the nature of the work he outlined for himself; a work so unique, elevated, and sublime that it could be clearly conceived, strongly grasped, and steadily held only by a supernatural mind. What was that work? He proposed the establishment on the earth, by the operation of purely moral forces, of a universal spiritual kingdom. A universal *spiritual* kingdom, I say. Men had dreamed before his time of universal kingdoms. The thought of a race community was not a new thought with Jesus, nor was it confined to that part of the world alone; whether consciously or unconsciously, the Babylonian kings had striven for a political union of all kingdoms; Alexander the Great dreamed of political unity; if Julius Cæsar did not distinctly propose a world empire, he did contemplate such an aggregation of the various political units as should secure the political hegemony of Rome; if Charlemagne did not dream of a universal kingdom, he did dream of a union of men in a political confederation as extensive as the continent of Europe. Men have dreamed of an intellectual kingdom that should be universal. It was the thought of Aristotle, and it is the thought of the most eminent thinker of our time on philosophical subjects, Mr. Herbert Spencer, who has for the dream and vision of his life the co-ordination of all truth into one vast universal and harmonious system that will explain all phenomena. The kingdom of Jesus is a spiritual kingdom; not an intellectual, not a political kingdom, but a kingdom in which the subjects are to be the conscious children of God, ruled by love, purity, truth, justice, righteousness, blossoming into high moral and spiritual experiences. It was to be the reign of God, as some one has strongly said, "in men, not over them." It is the new spiritual reign by which all men are to be re-molded and re-fashioned, created anew after the image of God. It is the final triumph of good and God over every form of moral and physical evil. It is to be universal in fact and in time; it is to embrace all men, and through these men all institutions, all governments, all industries, all literatures, all art, all policies, all traditions; it is to be universal in point of time—it is to be an ever-growing, never-ending kingdom. Other kingdoms shall wax and wane, and at last perish from off the face of the earth. This kingdom shall go on forever; its highest glories, its most magnificent victories, are reserved for a higher life and a purely spiritual sphere.

This kingdom was to make its way in the world by the operation of purely moral forces. Its King distinctly repudiated the use of coercion; the aid of government is not to be invoked. "Master, shall we call down fire from heaven to burn them up?" "Ye know not what manner of spirit ye are of!" "Peter, put up thy sword." Not by any physical force is this kingdom to be founded or finally established. How, then? Be good; let your light shine; win men by love; serve others; lose your own life; serve those most who need you most; bow yourself down, be like him, wait, be patient; the times and the seasons are his, and he shall yet be all in all.

What a work! How petty seem the projects of

Alexander and Napoleon! No such work was ever before conceived by mortal mind. An acute American thinker, Horace Bushnell, tells us that upon this single fact in Christ's life a profound German scholar, Reinhard, constructs a most powerful and convincing argument for the supernaturalness of Jesus. He went into a formal review of all the great founders of states, all the great lawgivers, all the prophet-founders of religions, all the philosophers, all the wise kings, and found as a fact that this idea of Jesus had never before been taken up by any living character in history. And yet, at thirty years of age, it is the easy and familiar thought of a Galilean artisan; at thirty years of age, with such a thought he is not ostentatious or vain; nor does he parade it, as geniuses are wont to exhibit their intellectual children. Nor was he in haste. He said it was first a "seed"—yea, the smallest of all seeds; "first the blade, and then the ear, and after that the full corn in the ear." He never was ambitious; he never was feverish; he was calm, quiet, patient with this great thought.

It is precisely here that his intellectual greatness meets, blends with, and is swallowed up by his moral greatness. To conceive of such a thought requires more than acuteness, more than sagacity, more than training, more than worldly wisdom; it requires a mind of a peculiar moral tone! I may employ a term more and more coming into use and significance, and say that the intellect must be "ethicalized" before it can see such visions, or dream such dreams, or think such thoughts. No one could dream of this kingdom unless he believed that love was mightier than penalty, right stronger than force ; the thought of such a kingdom could not be believed except by a heart open to the truth of the cross—that is, that the immeasurable power of God is to be sought in the capacity of his love to suffer.

The great sage of China, Confucius, toward the close of his long and illustrious career, said one day to his disciples, as they gathered about him, " I suppose that in letters I am equal to other men ; but the character of the perfect man, carrying out in his conduct what he professes, *is what I have not yet attained to.*" Did Jesus ever speak in that way? Did he ever confess lack of attainment? Did he ever say that he failed to realize his own ideal? Did he ever acknowledge that he failed to carry out in his conduct what he professed in his words? Where is the indication that he ever shrank or faltered from the solemn declaration of his absolute sinlessness? He stood in the midst of the men of his time, and said, " Which of you convinceth me of sin?" Who has convinced him of sin? Was he not sinless? If sin touched him, how? where? Was he merciless? Was he ambitious? Was he selfish? Was he wickedly angry? Was he not just, righteous, and true? Moreover, when did he need to spur himself to duty? When was it necessary for him to revive his flagging spirit in its love of righteousness? He needed to sustain his body, but *where* did he begin to break down ethically? If he spoke a false word, *where* is the word? If he exhibited an unholy temper, *where* did he exhibit it? If he was selfish, *where* was he so? If he asked others to do what he did not fulfill himself, *when* and *where* did he ask them to do it? I appeal to his enemies! Have they ever found one speck of moral impurity, one indication of selfishness, one single act of willfulness, one slight deviation from absolute rectitude! If they have, his perfect holiness is gone, and the King of the new kingdom is dethroned, for he built his kingship upon the deep and necessary truth that that which he exacted of all men he fulfilled in his own conduct and life. And they answer not! It is neither a Parker, nor a Strauss, nor a Renan, nor even an Ingersoll who has ever attempted to convict him of disloyalty, of self-seeking, of impurity, for he is holy, harmless, undefiled, and separate from sinners. How happens it, then, that he not only appeared as the custodian of this great and divine idea, but that he, and he alone, has succeeded in presenting himself to men as the pure, radiant, spotless, perfect Being, who has ever appeared in the history of the worlds?

We return to the well-known conditions of his life. Consider who he was in his family, his work, his social and intellectual environment; consider where he lived for thirty years, consider all the untoward circumstances of his early life, and then attempt to account for his mighty work and being by hypotheses of his humanity! Stand now in his presence with your theories of a great prophet, a great moral genius, a great religious reformer! How does it happen that such a being, under such circumstances, had this great, supreme, all embracing idea, and was continuously loyal to it? How does it happen that from the carpenter's bench in a small village, in a degraded province of a despised country, one came out to the world and thralled— not the feeble men, not the weak nations, but beginning with Paul, and going to Greece and Rome, he comes down the centuries, erecting his cross everywhere among the strong and robust nations. The torpid and decaying nations of the slumberous East might indeed allow him to pass by, but how are we to account for the fact that the aggressive, conquering, liberty-loving, duty-serving peoples of the continent of Europe, the great tribes that settled the West, the great Teutonic stock especially, the nations that rule the world, should be so influenced by his life and love and righteousness that they should worship him as God? What is the explanation?

The answer is that supernatural thoughts were natural to him, because he was a supernatural being; divine ideas were familiar to him, because he was divine; he was sinless, because he was the Sinless One incarnate; he was calm, patient, confident of ultimate victory, because he was the Ancient of Days, whose goings forth had been from everlasting; because in his right hand he held all treasures of time; because he surely touched all secret springs of power and influence; because as a map, and as a picture, the ages and the consummations of eternity were open before him! "And the Jews marveled, saying, How knoweth this man letters, having never learned? Jesus answered them, and said, My doctrine is not mine, but his that sent me. If any man will do his will, he shall know of the doctrine, whether it be of God, or whether I speak of myself." "Philip saith unto him" (and we all say it with Philip), "Lord, show us the Father, and it sufficeth us. Jesus saith unto him, Have I been so long time with you, and yet hast thou not known me, Philip? he that hath seen me hath seen the Father." And so, at last do we cry out with Thomas, each for himself, "My Lord and my God!"

THE CALL OF ABRAHAM.

Now the Lord had said unto Abram, Get thee out of thy country, and from thy kindred, and from thy father's house, unto a land that I will show thee: and I will make of thee a great nation, and I will bless thee, and make thy name great; and thou shalt be a blessing: and I will bless them that bless thee, and curse him that curseth thee: and in thee shall all families of the earth be blessed.—Gen. xii, 1-3.

THESE words describe, in its divine aspects or relations, one of the most noteworthy and significant events in the world's history. This pivotal historic fact is the call of Abram to be the first clear witness to the divine unity, the Father of the Jewish people, and the Founder of the Jewish Church, out of which, in the end, the Christian Church should spring and develop, by whose agency and power in turn the kingdom of God among men should at last be realized. Truly, then, may this great fact be remarked as one of the pivotal points of Old World history. The purely temporal or secular side of this transaction carries in it nothing extraordinary or unique. It relates how Terah, the father of Abraham, started from Ur of the Chaldees, with his entire family, to settle anew in the land of Canaan. Even then, it seems, the star of empire was beginning to wend its way westward. The first considerable stage of their journey brought them as far as Haran, between the Tigris and Euphrates rivers, on the southern, or rather southwestern, slope of the Armenian Mountains, where Terah died. Then Abraham, inheriting the chieftainship of the tribe, and so the governance of the family, takes up and carries onward to a successful completion the unfulfilled purpose of his father. With Sarah, his wife, and Lot, his nephew, together with the slaves which they had gotten, and the substance which they had gathered, he journeyed to the land of Canaan, entering it from the north, by way of Damascus. No intimation is anywhere given that it was in obedience to a divine call that Terah set out on the migration to Canaan. In his movement we see or hear of no higher impelling force than the natural migratory instinct of the ancient Semitic chieftains. He may have thought the land freer, the ranges for his flocks wider and safer, the pasturage richer, and the water more plentiful, than in his native Mesopotamia. Not so with Abraham. The original purpose of his father doubtless had its effect upon his mind, but he heard also the voice of the heavenly Father, the solemn summons of Almighty God, saying, "Get thee out of thy country, and from thy kindred, and from thy father's house, unto a land that I will show thee: and I will make of thee a great nation, and I will bless thee, and make thy name great; and thou shalt be a blessing: and I will bless them that bless thee, and curse him that curseth thee: and in thee shall all families of the earth be blessed." We have for our study this evening, "The Call of Abraham," constituting, as it does, a pivotal point of Old World history.

1. Let us remark, in the beginning, its rich and vast historical significance. As we hastily glance at this Semitic chieftain yonder, there may not be much calculated to arouse our attention, or profoundly impress the historic imagination. Nevertheless, he is one of the dozen or two really great and potent men in the whole history of the race. He is the father of the Jewish people. As we stand and watch this Eastern caravan journeying westward to Palestine, let us not forget that we are in the presence of *the beginnings of Jewish history!* There is always something solemn, to a reflecting mind, in the beginning of a single human life, however humble and obscure that life may seem to our imperfect vision. How vastly is that solemnity deepened and augmented when we stand by the cradle of a mighty people!

How real, and simple, and natural is this national beginning. Contrast it with the grotesque and fabulous legends of gods and goddesses, enveloping the early records of other ancient peoples, as Egypt, Assyria, Babylon, Persia, Greece, and Rome. Abraham is a man; simply and truly a man; pretending to nothing more; one like his brethren in actual identity of nature; a *friend* of God, indeed, but not a god, and making no pretension to superhuman claims.

I have called him the father of the JEWISH people! And what a people! What a history was then beginning! The modern Jew may justly boast of the most ancient and distinguished lineage of any man on the earth! We are accustomed to think of the Papacy as an antique institution, and yet fourteen hundred years before the time of the great Gregory VII., Elijah the Tishbite, a prophet of Israel, was rebuking the apostate Ahab, and confronting the priesthood of Baal! We speak of Herodotus as the Father of History, but five hundred years before he began to collect the materials of his famous work David had touched his lyre, that "lyre which the nations heard entranced," and by which the shepherd boy of Bethlehem became the "unchallenged king of psalmody till time shall be no more." More than three hundred years before the first recorded Olympiad of the Greeks a Hebrew prophet was teaching the Jewish people the spiritual nature of sacrifice. "And Samuel said, Behold, to obey is better than sacrifice, and to hearken than the fat of rams." The venerable name of Homer seems to carry us back to the beginnings of poetry and literature, but the chivalric Moses had nobly identified himself and his fortunes with the slaves of Goshen four hundred years before the blind old bard of "Scio's rocky isle" had begun his immortal epic! The boasted names of Europe's proudest aristocracy seem but of yesterday when compared with the illustrious names of Hebrew history.

2. *The divine call and the peculiar training of Abraham, as recited in the Scriptures, should teach us the glory and the beauty of mercy, charity, and tol-*

eration. Abraham was at one and the same time a very imperfect but a very good man. He must be looked at largely, royally, generously, somewhat in the way in which God looks at men, or he will be sure to disappoint you. He was guilty of deceit, of culpable weakness, of mendacity, and of something akin to cruelty. Tried by our standards he would, of course, utterly fail. But on the other hand consider his virtues, his excellences, his strong points, his many meritorious qualities. Remember his unvarying courtesy; his kindness to Lot, the orphan nephew; his large unselfishness and generosity in dealing with him; his unsought, unpaid service to the King of Sodom; his touching and urgent intercession for the city of Sodom; his gracious hospitality; his wonderful faith in God; his quick, full, unhesitating, uncalculating obedience to God! When he was called to go to Canaan, he at once got ready and started. The very day on which he covenanted with God to keep his commandments, and walk in his ways, he circumcised his entire household, while in his offering of Isaac he most conspicuously exhibited a faith and obedience that approached the sublime!

Such was the strange mixture of elements in the character of Abraham. God's great mercy and wondrous loving-kindness overlooked his petty faults, while the divine charity dwelt with delight upon his virtues, and so it was that he became the father of the faithful. Alas! how differently we we often act in our judgments of men. We look long upon the weaknesses, the mistakes, the infirmities, the sins—we sometimes magnify them—while we not infrequently almost entirely overlook the virtues. No man is entirely faulty. Every man is sound and good somewhere. Along some line, in some range of power, in some element of disposition or character, every man has virtue, or the capacity for it. Hunt these nobler qualities up, and fix your attention upon them, if you mean to become imitators of God. We must learn to take men as they are, in this world, especially if we really mean to help them, and we should always remember that very imperfect men are sometimes very good men, even as David was a man after God's own heart.

The many-sidedness of Abraham's character should emphasize anew for us the much-needed lesson of toleration. His strengths and weaknesses, his merits and his faults, should teach us that *in the same human character, and at the same time*, good and evil may co-exist. His prayer for Sodom shows his compassion for wicked men. They were not even of his religion—they were idolaters. His service to the King of Sodom shows that he could help and rescue an alien, a heretic and an idolater, when in distress. There is nothing in him of the narrow and bitter spirit of intolerance shown by the Jews of a later time. Contrast his noble spirit in praying for Sodom with the desire of the disciples of Jesus to call down fire from heaven on the Samaritan villagers. There is nothing mean or petty

The Call of Abraham.

or dwarfing, nothing merely Jewish, about him. He seems to belong to the RACE. Such men as Abraham show us how divine and glorious a thing toleration really is, for without mutual forbearance and charity, I am sure, we will never be able to understand God's work in this world at all. A beautiful legend of the Talmud may possibly explain to us how in some vision of the night Abraham first learned the lesson of toleration. When one evening Abraham sat at his tent door, according to his custom, waiting to entertain strangers, he espied an old man, who seemed to be a hundred years of age, stooping and leaning on his staff, weary with age and travel, coming toward him. He received him kindly, washed his feet, provided supper, and caused him to sit down; but observing that the old man ate and prayed not, nor begged for a blessing on his meat, Abraham asked him why he did not worship the God of heaven. The old man told him that he worshiped the god of fire only, and acknowledged no other God; at which answer, Abraham grew so zealously angry that he thrust the old man out of his tent, and exposed him to all the evils of the night and an unguarded condition. When the old man was gone God called to Abraham, and asked him where the stranger was; he replied, "I thrust him away because he did not worship thee." God answered: "I have suffered him to live before me these hundred years, though he dishonored me; and thou couldst not endure him for a single night when he gave thee no trouble." Upon this Abraham fetched him back again, and gave him hospitable entertainment and wise instruction.

The story is a fable, a legend, I know, but the lesson is always needed. If God be so patient and tolerant of flaws and imperfections in a human character, as we see here in Abraham's case, should not we? And if of moral faults, how much more of mere intellectual error! These bad, mistaken, and wicked men and women all about us, God suffers them, and shall not we? My friends, it is better to pray even for Sodom than to curse it. There is only one thing God is unwilling to put into men's hands, and that is the infliction of retaliation. "Vengeance is MINE; I will repay, saith the Lord."

3. Consider the momentous import, from the stand-point of religious truth, of the call of Abraham. He was more than the father of the Jewish people, and the founder of the Jewish nation. He was the first clear, undoubted, divinely instructed witness to the unity, the spirituality, and the real governance of Jehovah. That is, he was the first witness to the actuality, the reality of a supernatural revelation. He was an organ for the expression of the divine will. He was inspired of God, fitted, taught, prepared by God, to be the medium of truth undiscoverable by man's unaided faculties. The simple idea of the divine unity, for example, is in the world. Men do believe in one Lord, not many gods. How did it get here? Whence its origin?

It is as a matter of fact distinctly traceable to the Jews as a people. Historically, we can trace it back step by step to this Jewish people. So, in like manner, we trace it back, generation by generation, family by family, until we find it in the family and person of Abraham. He unquestionably held it, and that antecedently to all others. The polytheism or idolatry then prevailing among his contemporaries, in one country not only, but in all the world, is now universally conceded. Whence, then, did he derive this peculiar idea, this sacred truth? He entirely escaped the worship of the heavenly bodies, and the deification of eminent men, as priests and kings. Somehow or other, he, and he alone, is wholly free from every taint of idolatry. Again I say, Abraham is in clear and undoubted possession of this idea, and I press the solemn question, " Whence did he derive it?" And I answer, *God himself revealed it to him by his Spirit.* The greatest living Oriental scholar, the chief of those who make comparative religion a study, Max Müller, says, " And if we were asked how this one Abraham passed through the denial of all other gods to the knowledge of the one true God, we are content to answer that it was by a special divine revelation."

O the blessed significance of it! O glorious word! God has spoken to us! The silences have been broken, and the loving messages of God have come to us, bidding us look up, and live, and hope! We know not the distance between the summerland of God's heart and these wastes of sin, but it has been traversed by God's angels of mercy, and will be again. The words of the Eternal have been spoken to man. Abraham has heard these words, and is henceforth the Pilgrim of the Invisible!

LAW IN THE SPIRITUAL REALM.

If ye keep my commandments, ye shall abide in my love; even as I have kept my Father's commandments, and abide in his love.—John xv, 10.

MAN is the subject of law throughout his entire earthly existence. He never escapes its rule for a single instant. There is a cause, a reason, a law for his first and for his last breath. He is what he is from moment to moment by virtue of his obedience or disobedience to the conditions environing him. He is related to the physical globe, to the air, to the light, to the heat, to food, to work, to society, to play, to trade, to commerce, to government, to his fellow-men, and the laws of these various relations are necessary to his existence, growth, happiness, and power. In other words, we have our existence in a moral universe. The constitution under which we live is such that if one event occurs another event necessarily occurs. The constitution of affairs is such that consequent must have its antecedent, that every effect must have a cause, that what *is* is the child of the past and the parent of the future; that all results, whether they be gross and material, or fine, spiritual, and impalpable, are conditioned, and not whimsical, or arbitrary, or capricious.

The solemn message of nature to man is: "Keep my commandments, and I will bless you, I will feed you, I will support and sustain you, I will elevate, strengthen, enrich, and honor you. Disobey my laws, and I will punish you, I will weaken you, I will give you pain, I will degrade you, I will make you poor, and at last I will destroy you." This is the impartial, unvarying message of nature to man every-where, in all ages and in all countries, in savagery and in civilization.

All we have comes primarily from the earth. Out of the soil comes, first or last, that which supports human life, and that without which human life could not be maintained on this globe; but here, as everywhere, law reigns. We avail ourselves of the products and wealth of the earth by ascertaining and obeying certain well-established laws. It is not a matter of indifference when a man plants corn or sows wheat; there are times for doing those things, and our business is to ascertain these times, to conform to these conditions; and any attempt to go contrary to these immutable conditions of nature leaves us without corn and without wheat. The man who should attempt to do in the month of December that which nature has appointed to be done in the month of May, the man who should attempt to do in the month of May that which should be done in the month of October, would speedily find that law reigns in husbandry, and that it is only by finding out and conforming to the conditions of germination and growth on the physical globe that we can have our life on the earth. If we do not obey these conditions, instantly we suffer loss; and if to-day the whole race should deliberately resolve to set aside these conditions, and every man proceed to live after his own sweet will, the time would not be long before man would perish by starvation.

So is it when we come to our bodies; there is a cause for our health or our ill health. There are laws governing the growth, the strength, the health, the longevity of all physical organisms on this globe. When the headache comes, if you have reached the period of intelligence and reflection, you at once begin to inquire as to the cause of the disturbance. You know that the pain did not come arbitrarily, or fortuitously, or vindictively, or capriciously; you know that there must be some near or remote cause for it, either in what you ate or did not eat, in the loss of sleep, in extraordinary exertions, or in your inheritances—you are certain that somewhere or other there is a distinct cause or reason for the headache. There is a cause for the fever; there is a cause for the cough; there is a cause for the pestilence; there are conditions, laws, surrounding our physical being, and it is at our grave peril that we seek to evade or escape from them. Obedience to them is the price we pay for health, strength, and long life.

The reign of law obtains in all the commercial and industrial pursuits and activities of human life.

"Well, young man," says the gray-haired head of the house to the new employee, "do you know the laws of success in this business?" "Not very well, sir." "In the first place, you must be industrious, you must be thrifty, you must be economical, you must be clear-headed and sagacious, you must be diligent, you must be honest, you must be patient." In other words, the laws of industry, of patience, of skill, of sagacity, of economy, constitute the conditions of commercial and industrial success. If any young man, swollen with vanity, imagines that law does not rule here, let him try it: let him be lazy, let him be improvident and wasteful, let him be careless of his word, let it be a matter of indifference with him whether he shall arrive at his office at ten o'clock in the morning or two o'clock in the afternoon, and he will soon find that, although these laws are not printed in any statute-book, nevertheless they determine the question of success in all the industrial and commercial relations of life.

Law conditions the awakening and unfolding of the intellectual powers and the acquisition of knowledge. Grote's *History of Greece*, twelve good-sized volumes, may be enough to discourage the beginner, but he who would have a broad and thorough knowledge of Greek history must read it, and master its contents. You cannot dream yourself into a knowledge of it, you cannot wish yourself into a knowledge of it; there is only one way to be familiar with the glorious age of Pericles, and that is thoroughly to read about it, and meditate about it, and reflect about it, and thus get yourself steeped in the very spirit of the time. Suppose the young collegian or student has a rich social nature, he cannot give full vent to this nature and become an exact and broad scholar: he must say to his strong social desires, "You must serve and wait." Law governs the acquisition of all knowledge, as well as the sharpening and drilling into fineness and power of our faculties. There is no easy, royal, luxurious road to learning; there is no royal road to wealth; there is no royal road to health; all these ways have been thoroughly explored for centuries, and they who attempt to acquire knowledge, or to amass wealth, or to build up strong bodies by violating these laws are sure to come to grief and ruin. The man has never lived who has been able, in the presence of these inexorable facts, to set up an ideal universe of his own. Law rules from the time we begin to breathe until all is over; and then law takes our bodies and decomposes them, and restores the elements that entered into them to their original form, that they may in turn enter into other bodies. We were born, we work, we love, we suffer, we triumph, we fail, we die, under the reign of impartial, immutable, beneficent law.

And now, when we come to the life and activities of the spirit, does God reverse his method? When we come to the realm of the religious life, with its rich experiences and glorious products, has God given us a lawless, chance, haphazard realm? When we come to that sphere in which we ascertain man's relations and duties to those things that are invisible, is law banished? Do we say that caprice, impulse, and fancy rule here? Is such teaching in accordance with the ascertained analogies of the development of human nature, and the maintenance of human life in other realms of activity? Man is not only the subject of physical conditions; he is not only related to the state, and to trade, and to the intellectual life; he is related also (and far more deeply than he imagines) to the spiritual realm; he is related to the great truth of an Invisible Father, whose child he is, and whose nature he bears, and upon his spirit is the ineffaceable divine impress. He is tied to great and solemn duties, from which he may not escape, and which it is his glory to acknowledge and to perform; duties that suggest and involve eternity. He sustains relations to the great idea of the survival of his life hereafter and forever, and so of a more intimate and perfect knowledge of the Father of his spirit. Can it be possible that we are in the vise-like grip of law until we touch that realm, and that then fancy, arbitrariness, luck, accident, are to take the place of law? And yet I fear that many religious people indulge themselves in the luxurious delusion that the religious realm is lawless; without order, without fixed conditions, without distinct and stringent requirements of obedience. Hear the text again: "If ye keep my commandments, ye shall abide in my love." Where is it taught otherwise in the Bible? This passage does not say, "If ye keep my commandments, I will *begin* to love you." It is not taught here that the love of Jesus Christ to men as the expression, the manifestation, the bodying forth of the eternal love of God, is contingent upon our obedience to him, but it is taught that if we are to realize that love, if we are consciously to enter into it, if we are to abide in it, we must keep his commandments. The statement is not, " Obey, that you may create this divine love," but, " Obey, that you may know it, and abide in it," and the difference is vast and significant. " If ye keep my commandments, ye shall abide in my love; even as I have kept my Father's commandments, and abide in his love."

Now, what are some of the plain, simple commandments of Jesus? You know he did not give us just so many precepts after the letter, he did not give us ceremonial ritual commandments after the example of Moses to the Jews, but, nevertheless, he gave us commandments. I may not exhaust them in the brief time at my disposal, but I can indicate and emphasize some of them.

It will not be disputed that this is one of his commandments: REPENT! Repent instantly, repent thoroughly, repent strenuously—all men will agree that this was, and is, one of his commandments. He began to preach by saying: " Repent; change your lives; fall out with evil; turn away from the evil that you find in yourself; do not waste your life in meditating about it, but turn away from wrong-doing at once, for the kingdom of heaven is at hand, it is here now, it is open to all who will enter it; put down the evil that is within you, flee at once from the evil that solicits you; remodel your dispositions; set your faces toward that which is good." How can a man expect to discern and enter into Christ's love who has never repented? How can a man expect to abide in Christ's love, as the dearest possession of his soul, who has never been willing to conform to this commandment of repentance? This love which is so freely proffered to us, and is disclosed as divine and eternal, how can the unrepentant man avail himself of it? If he will not repent, or if he repents only of those sins that are easy to repent of, if he will repent of those sins which are superficial and external only, and not of those sins which are internal and spiritual: if he will not repent of the malign spirit of envy that eats out the heart of love and holiness, if he will not repent of the selfishness that is mastering him, if he will not cast out the whole infernal brood of inner devils that are surely demonizing him—if he will not repent of all these things how can he expect to abide in that Love which has for the first and fundamental condition of its realization the earnestness and entireness of our repentance?

PRAYER is a command of Jesus. Not that we shall formally repeat so many prayers a definite number of times each day, not that our prayers shall be of a certain length, not that we shall include such and such topics, not that we shall pray at such and such holy places, in a given attitude, but this general truth is his commandment concerning prayer: that man needs to carry his spirit up to God, that it may be cleansed and refreshed, and receive the divine light. This also does he teach and command us concerning prayer: that we are to be diligent, intelligent, and persistent in it; that we ought not to faint or be discouraged in cultivating the spirit and habit of prayer; that if the unjust judge, by reason of unceasing importunity, would do right, how much more may we expect the Just Judge to do right when his children cry day and night unto him? How, then, can a man expect to abide in the love of Jesus, to enter into the enjoyment and strength of that love, who does not pray? How can a man expect to abide in it who *says* prayers? I am not now referring to those persons of other religious denominations who use fixed forms of prayer. I speak of the religious man who is in such a hurry in the morning that he has no time for private prayer, unless it be to mumble a few unfelt, superstitious words, and omits the family worship after breakfast! I speak of the man who at night gives hours to recreation and amusement, and grudges minutes for God! Call that prayer! Call that taking the soul out of its life of sordid care, and out of all that which defiles and degrades, and lifting it up into rapt and holy and blessed communion with God! How can a man expect to know the love of God in Christ, if he will not daily strive to live in the atmosphere of prayer?

Another commandment of Christ may be comprehended in the general expression, *strenuousness of spiritual endeavor*. A Christian life may be made easy, luxurious, and self-indulgent, in view of the prevailing idea of superficial expansion and culture, but when I turn to the New Testament, and open my whole heart and mind to the real meaning and spirit of the Book, I am more and more impressed with one thing: that Jesus Christ commands us strenuously to endeavor toward the spiritual life. What does he say? "STRIVE to enter in at the strait gate; for many, I say unto you, will seek to enter in and shall not be able." We may imagine that it is a delightful holiday task to live a Christian life amid the abounding wealth and luxury of a great city; but it is not a holiday task to live a Christian life here or anywhere if the New Testament be our book of directions. If we would indeed live that life, it will require of us the most urgent, the most through, the most persistent, the most strenuous endeavors of which we are capable. How shall we know the love of God if we are strangers to this intense, fervid, spiritual earnestness?

Consider the great commandment of Jesus: the commandment to cultivate the disposition of love toward all men. I reserved it for the last, because it is the commanding commandment of Jesus. I know how we evade it; I know how we seek to escape from it; I know how disagreeable it is to the carnal and worldly spirit. But if Jesus did not command men to love men; if he did not command men so to love each other that they would not hate, or wrong, or defile, or degrade each other; if he did not teach me to love all men, without regard to their culture, or their color, or their wealth, or their poverty, or their virtue, or their weakness; if Jesus Christ does not teach me that I am to love all men as men, if he does not teach me that I am to put up with disagreeable people, if he does not teach me to bear with mean people, if he does not teach me that my whole heart's love is to go out to men in proportion to the sharpness and greatness of their need, if he does not teach me that my life is to be lived in this atmosphere of love for men—if he does not command and teach me these things, he has not commanded or taught me any thing. How, then, can a man expect to rise up to the knowledge of this divine love who does not love men, and is not trying to love men?

These are some of the conditions upon which we are to know and abide in the divine love. There is no room, then, in the Christian life for fanaticism; there is no place left in the Christian life for that kind of false enthusiasm which expects the end without the means. Not a few people are just religious enough to be unhappy and miserable all the time. They are like a bright boy I knew at college, the son of a wealthy and prominent man, while nearly all the other students were of the homespun sort, and came from plain and humble homes. He was naturally as well endowed as any of the students, perhaps better endowed, but the truth was that he did not want to study; he wanted to be at the head of his class without work; he wanted, without toil and self-denial, to pass the great rude boy that came from the country—a boy who made his first appearance at college with no collar on, and with the roughest pair of boots and the shortest pair of trousers ever worn by a prospective freshman. When he saw *that* boy going to the head of the class he was irritated and exasperated; he had just enough desire to be a scholar to keep himself in a state of misery all the time, and all because he would not obey the laws of college mastery and leadership. How many people there are who are religious in that way! They are complaining and murmuring all the time, and yet they will not keep the laws of the Christian life. It is just as it is elsewhere—in the practice of the law, in business life, in teaching school, every-where: hanging on to every pursuit and vocation in life is a great crowd of murmurers, whiners, complainers, fault-finders. There are men who sit in their offices (where, by the way, nobody ever comes to see them), who can tell you exactly how that man across the street made his millions, but they never tell you why they did not make millions. They rail at the world because they have not succeeded, when the reason of it is that they have been idle, or dishonest, or self-indulgent, and have not brought to bear upon their work in life sufficient energy and discretion. So there are people in the church who are leading miserable religious lives: they never have any joy; they never have any discernible spiritual power; it is all a question of disagreeable duty with them; they perform certain religious duties because the set time has come for their observance, and because they think in a vague way that if they do not do these things some great, undefined, awful calamity will happen to them. They want to secure the peace and power of the love of Christ without keeping his commandments; they want life, and comfort, and faith, but they are not willing to obey the commandments. Repent! "I will repent of every thing but that one thing, and I wont repent of that now." Pray? "Well, I am a busy man, and I have not time for family prayers; I am willing to *say* my prayers morning and evening." "Strenuousness of spiritual endeavor?" They know nothing at all about strenuousness of spiritual endeavor. "Cultivating a disposition of love toward all men?" Why, they despise and sneer at the majority of men! Now, how can one, so living, expect to know the love of Christ? "If ye keep my commandments, ye shall abide in my love; even as I have kept my Father's commandments, and abide in his love."

Our obedience does not create, but it brings us into the conditions in which, and in which alone, we can clearly discern and joyfully appropriate the divine love. I once lived in a State where there were a great many lazy and ignorant farmers, culpably ignorant of the properties of the soil, and of what kind of crops could most successfully be raised by them. Suppose a farmer in this region who spent most of his time hunting and trying to get food for twelve or thirteen lean, lank, hungry dogs which he kept, and who was always complaining that the soil was so poor that he could scarcely get a living out of it. Suppose such a man as this should wake up some morning and find out that what he needed to do was to obey the conditions of success—namely, to plow his fields; even, if the soil was a little poor, to plow deep, and not merely scratch the surface of the ground; that he was to take out the briars and weeds by the roots, to have secure fences, so as to keep the cattle and hogs out, to sow good seed and diligently cultivate it, and that by so doing he should avail himself of the air and light and heat and rain, and all the producing properties of the soil. Imagine such a man, after he had raised two or three generous crops, complacently saying to himself: "I created the sun; I created the light; I caused the rain to fall; I created the constituent elements in the soil that gave me my wheat." That is what some people would have us say about the love of our Father in heaven; they want us to say that when we get to doing good we create in him for the first time a disposition to love us. In other words, that when we begin to do good God begins to love us, and that if the case were otherwise God would not love us at all. No, no, my brethren. The divine love for men existed long before we were born; it has existed from the beginning—if any body knows when that was. By obedience (and it is his love even that inclines us to obedience) we bring ourselves into conditions where that love becomes present, actual, realizable. I notice that when my boy disobeys me, he seems to have serious doubts as to the reality of my love for him. If I attempt, in a practical way, to convince him that I love him, he does not hesitate openly to deny the fact of my love. Do we not all know that a child, during the period of its defiant willfulness, will accept no outward evidences of parental love? And do we not all know that obedience to Christ's commandments is an indispensable condition of making his love real and present to our hearts?

When Thomas Carlyle determined to write the *Life of Frederick the Great* he put himself in training to realize, as far as possible, all the conditions of the life of Prussia at that time. He prepared his room with reference to it; the desk on which he wrote was from Germany; his inkstand was from Germany; his ink was from Germany; his pen was from Germany; the paper on which he wrote was from Germany; the pictures on the walls were German pictures; all the books in that room were German books, and related to that time; so that when he went into the room at any time to compose he was in the presence of such circumstances as served perpetually to suggest Germany to his mind, and he almost lived in that room during the years in which he produced that great book.

This age is spiritually decrepit; halting, languid, feeble. It is a time, indeed, in which there is much to praise, a time of discovery of great truths, of vast external works of benevolence, but it is not an age of profound spiritual life. It is an age of feet, not wings. It is not an age when the great invisible realities are strongly grasped and realized by men; it is an age in which we *hope* that life may have a spiritual meaning; it is an age in which we *hope* there may be a personal, willing, loving God; it is an age in which we *hope* there may be life to come; but it is not an age in which these great supersensuous truths are steadily realized and made potential in the lives of men. And no wonder; no wonder! We have not obeyed the conditions by which we realize spiritual truth. When the men of this age will repent; when they will repent instantly and thoroughly; when the men of this time will PRAY, not *say prayers;* when the men of this time engage themselves to strenuousness of spiritual endeavor; when the men of this time will learn to love all their brother-men, not by machinery, not by charity societies, not by subscribing to the support of the Gospel, but by downright kindness and helpfulness— when we thus fulfill the conditions of spiritual penetration and vigor, there will come to the men of this time an experience of the power and the blessedness of the great invisible realities! O how poor and empty are our lives! You may amass your wealth, you may acquire your knowledge, you may establish your fame, you may have the love of wife and child, but who does not know that there come passages, histories, experiences, griefs in life, when not wealth, nor knowledge, nor ambition, nor the love of wife, or child, or friend, will satisfy the desolate soul? Who does not know that there come times when, above all things else, we yearn to know that there is a Mighty One to love us? Who does not know that there are times when what we need to know is, not whether we love God, but whether God loves us? And how can we know it if we will not heed his commandments? This is the fatal heresy: to deny the reign of law in things spiritual. May we be preserved from this heresy! May God mercifully incline our wayward hearts to keep his commandments, to the end that we may know and eternally abide in his righteous, sovereign Love!

THE REASONABLENESS OF IMMORTALITY.

I.

If a man die, shall he live again?—Job xiv, 14.

THIS is an ancient, universal, and solemn question. It is an ancient question, I say; for we may well suppose that the first man who ever stood upon the earth, when he found himself in the dread presence of death, asked this question. It is a universal question; for we may well suppose that every man who since that time has entered, or has seen his friends entering, the valley of the shadow of death, has asked the same question. It is a solemn question; for we cannot suppose that any normally constituted man, any sound, honest, healthy moral nature, could ask or seek to answer this question in a spirit of mere intellectual levity. It is, further, more a question of immense and inconceivable practical importance. If this question is answered in the affirmative, if it be declared by some competent and reliable authority that man shall live again after death, a new light and radiance and inspiration is shed over the pathway and experiences of human life, while the opening vistas of the untrodden future are invested with a sweet attractiveness and a divine glory. If this question be answered in the negative, if it be declared by some competent and reliable authority that death ends all, what is this life of ours but one continued round of anguish and sorrow, of unsatisfied yearnings and bitter disappointments? If, to use the language of Professor Tyndall in his famous Belfast address, "you and I are destined, like streaks of the morning cloud, to melt into the infinite azure of the past," life is a golden and glorious promise never to be fulfilled. If man is not immortal, nature "has imposed upon her sons, and made them a lie." We have been created to be baffled, to be thwarted, to be mocked, to be toyed with, by the great blind, pitiless forces of nature, and then to be dissolved into nothingness forever. Christianity teaches that man shall live again after death. It sings no funereal hymns, it wails no requiems, it chants no dirges. Distinctly and eloquently and solemnly does it proclaim the truth of our great immortality. It adopts and makes its own the sentiment of the poet:

> "The sun is but a spark of fire,
> A transient meteor in the sky;
> The soul, immortal as its sire,
> Shall *never* die."

We are to consider the reasonableness of the Christian doctrine of a conscious future life for the human spirit. It is not my purpose to attempt to *prove*, by any methods of formal logic, that the soul shall survive death. The evidences of the reality and permanence of our spiritual being are neither logical nor physical, but moral and personal. The reality of a future life does not depend upon the mere strength of an argument. As Christians, we believe in immortality because Jesus Christ, who came out from God, bringing with him the disclosure of the eternal will of God, hath abolished death and brought life and immortality to light. Upon this Rock we build our hopes. The question proposed now is, Is this doctrine of Christianity credible and reasonable? Are they not irrational who question and deny this great truth? We teach that this doctrine is confirmed by the highest reason, that it is in harmony with a spiritual interpretation of nature, and that it is in sympathy with the indisputable facts of man's manifold being.

There is one preliminary consideration worthy of serious attention as we enter upon our study of this subject, and that is the impossibility of establishing the negative proposition. No man now living, and no man who ever will live, can show that there is no future life for the soul. It is both physically and intellectually impossible.

1. Before it can be declared with any degree of confidence, or, rather, before it can be declared without the most arrogant intellectual presumption, that the immortal life of the soul is a dream and a fancy, the entire universe of God must be exhaustively explored. No man can declare that disembodied spirits do not exist until he has penetrated into every nook and corner of the universe and found no such spirits. He must be able to show

that no such forms of life have an existence, and he must be able to show it in an entirely satisfactory manner. His exploration of the universe must not be partial, it must be exhaustive. He must be able to scale its inaccessible heights, to sound its unfathomable depths, to measure all its infinite spaces, before he can be even a competent witness. He must have visited and have scrutinized every portion of the creation of Almighty God. Not our earth, and sun, and system only, not the planetary spaces only, not the fixed stars only, not the stellar spaces only, not the Milky Way only, but all suns, all stars, all nebulæ, all space. It will not do for this explorer to return after having visited ninety-nine parts of the universe, and declare that no disembodied souls can be found, for they may have their dwelling-place in the one part unvisited and unexplored. Nothing short of an exhaustive exploration of the universe would justify the denial of the existence of glorified human spirits. But such an exploration is physically impossible. The universe, like its majestic and inscrutable Author, is infinite and unsearchable. No man now living, no man who ever will live, can explore and exhaust the infinite creation of the infinite God.

2. But suppose such an exploration could actually be made. The declaration of the explorer that he found no translated and disenthralled souls of men would not justify the conclusion that no such souls existed. It is possible, yea, it is highly probable, that he would not be possessed of powers and

faculties sufficiently fine and discriminating to enable him to perceive, discern, or touch a spirit. Philosophers generally concede that matter possesses, or may possess, many qualities of which we are at present ignorant, on account of the grossness and heaviness of our faculties. If we had finer, sharper, more penetrating powers, we might be able greatly to extend our list of the qualities and properties of matter. As, by practice, we whet and sharpen our faculties, as we improve the instruments we employ in the study of matter, new and astonishing discoveries are made of its qualities and powers. Now, if our faculties are too gross and heavy to perceive all the qualities of matter, is it at all probable that they are sufficiently fine and powerful to discern disembodied spirits? We know nothing of the forms, modes, activities of spirit life. We can form no tangible or sensible conception of a pure spirit. We know very little of mind or spirit, even when localized in matter. We know nothing at all about it when, separated from matter, it is free and untrammeled. Spirits may be near us, or they may be afar off. We know nothing of their mode of life or locomotion. The spirit life may be as near to our life as the waves of the ocean to the shore, or it may be removed from us at an immeasurable and inconceivable distance. Spirits elude the grasp of all our faculties. They are too unworldly, too subtle, too ethereal, to readily surrender themselves to our examination. Now our explorer might have visited the outermost confines of creation, he might have carefully scrutinized all the intervening spaces, but how convincing would be his testimony? The question would immediately arise, Did he possess the faculties requisite for the discernment of a spirit? He may have traveled through densely peopled regions of spirits, and missed them all because of coarseness of faculty. If his powers had been finer and sharper, he might, perhaps, have discovered spirits. His testimony would, therefore, be valueless; at least, it could not be decisive of a question of such profound importance.

Whoever would successfully deny the existence of a future state must possess perfect faculties, and the power to visit and examine the entire material universe. Now, no man possesses either; no man ever will possess either. Therefore, it is impossible for any man ever to prove that there is no future life.

The negative being impossible to establish, let us inquire into the reasonableness of the affirmative.

1. A strong presumption in favor of immortality is raised by the significance of the universal longing after it. The fact that all men have longed for a future life is not denied. Their conceptions of the hereafter may often have been crude, coarse, barbaric, materialistic. Very few of the elements of immortality as we conceive of it may have entered into the minds of savage men. Nevertheless, the savage has longed for a new life in the dim hereafter. This longing has been universal. The great

and the humble, the cultured and the coarse, the gifted and the stolid, the rich and the poor, the strong and the weak, the scholar and the boor, the king and the slave, the poet and the hod-carrier, the Greek poet and the sensuous barbarian, the English philosopher and the negroes of equatorial Africa, have all alike looked up to the stars and longed for a home beyond them. To the reflective and thoughtful mind this fact is full of significance, suggestion, and prophecy. By this fact the race has all along been testifying to its sense of the narrowness, the incompleteness, and the defectiveness of the present life, and the eminent desirableness of another life where all things shall be rounded out to completeness, wholeness, and harmony. Has the race been mistaken? Is this life a perfect one? Is there nothing fragmentary about it? Do we not feel that it is incomplete? With all its joy, and beauty, and work, and growth, and culture, and love, are we not perpetually dreaming of a life more joyous, with a finer, loftier, richer beauty, with frictionless work, with more rapid growth, with a more genial and perfect culture, with a higher and less selfish love? Here, then, is a race, confessedly imperfect, longing with passionate fervor for perfection, and, if death destroys our being, heartlessly denied this perfection by the very Being who himself implanted the desire. For, if man is not to complete this life hereafter, why was he created capable of conceiving of a hereafter? Why should he be endowed with this fervor of perfection if it is never to be realized? If death ends all, and justice is to be done, man should have been so constituted as not to be able to peer anxiously into the future in the vain hope that the bright, consummate flower of existence should then unfold in perfect beauty. God is not to be charged with the infinite cruelty of thus mocking, baffling, and cheating the whole human race. The very outreach of our souls after immortality is, under the rule of a moral Deity, a pledge and a prophecy that the coveted destiny shall be ours.

2. The desire for immortality grows in fineness, purity, fervency, and power with the advancing intelligence and increasing culture of the human race. This desire was not one of the world's childhood only. The world has had its childhood beliefs and desires. In its childhood the world believed that every stream had its naiad and every forest its dryad. It believed that the earth was a flat surface, that the sun was a comparatively insignificant body, and that it moved round the earth as its humble servant. It believed that the earth was made in six literal days of twenty-four hours each. All these beliefs, and many similar ones, the world has outgrown, or is rapidly outgrowing. It is true, also, that in the world's childhood men believed in immortality. The early man, wandering from pasture to pasture with his flock of sheep and goats, was also seeking a better country, that is, a heavenly. Scarce ever did the homeless pilgrim, in the freshness of the early dawn, strike his tent, and

prepare for another day's march, that he did not yearn for a permanent home; that he did not long for the air of a bright eternal morning; that he did not dream of a city which had foundations, whose maker and builder was God! But the world has not outgrown its early faith in, and passionate longing for, a life free from evil, pain, and strife. Now in its manhood, strong, vigorous, aggressive, its faith in a compensating future is more vitalizing and tenacious than ever. Nor is it true that this desire has been confined to ignorant, timid, slavish, and superstitious peoples. The lowly, the crude, the undeveloped, the uncivilized, have, indeed, desired this precious boon. They have hoped that heaven would right the wrongs of earth, and they have waited with patience and hope for the righteous and solemn retributions of eternity. The untutored savage of the tropical forests, the serpent worshiper of Bengal, the wild red man, who once proudly claimed this continent as his own, all have sought with avidity the rounding out of their being in a more congenial clime. So have the choicest spirits of the race. Abraham, Moses, Job, Isaiah, Paul, Socrates, Plato, Aristotle, Demosthenes, Æschylus, Seneca, Cicero, Marcus Aurelius, Epictetus, Dante, Da Vinci, Goethe, Schiller, Jean Paul, Lessing, Kant, Shakespeare, Milton, Haydn, Handel, Mozart, Beethoven, Addison, Johnson, Cowper, Burke, Macaulay, Froude, Tennyson, and Buckle, all have *desired* immortality. As life grows in complexity, as men more and more come to themselves, as our wants increase, as our channels of pleasure and sources of culture multiply, as all our faculties become finer, sharper, more distinct, and more fruitful—in short, as man advances toward the ripeness and consummation of his being—the desire for a freer, fuller, ampler life grows in fervency and power. The more a man becomes a man, the greater is his dread of extinction. The growth of the race, the increase and enlargement of its knowledge, is, and ever has been, accompanied by an increase of desire for immortality. And what is true of the race is true also of the individual. To deny immortality is evidence of immaturity, of superficiality, of lack of depth and patience of thought. Intellectual growth is almost invariably marked by a rejection of materialism, and the gradual acceptance of the great truth that spirit forces are supreme in the universe. Bryant at nineteen did not sing of immortality as he did at eighty-two. Here is the doubting, hesitating, almost pagan poetry of his youth:

> "So live, that when thy summons comes to join
> The innumerable caravan which moves
> To that mysterious realm where each shall take
> His chamber in the silent halls of death,
> Thou go not, like the quarry-slave at night,
> Scourged to his dungeon, but, sustained and soothed
> By an unfaltering trust, approach thy *grave*
> Like one who wraps the drapery of his couch
> About him, and lies down to pleasant dreams."

Here is the high and solemn hope that animated his verse at eighty-two:

"What is there beyond?
Hear what the wise and good have said. Beyond
That belt of darkness still the years roll on,
More gently, but with not less mighty sweep.
They gather up again and softly bear
All the sweet lives that late were overwhelmed
And lost to sight, all that in them was good,
Noble, and truly great, and worthy love,
The lives of infants and ingenious youths,
Sages and saintly women who have made
Their households happy; all are raised and borne
By that great current in its onward sweep,
Wandering and rippling with caressing waves
Around green islands fragrant with the breath
Of flowers that never wither. So they pass
From stage to stage along the shining course
Of that bright river, broadening like a sea.
As its smooth eddies curl along their way
They bring old friends together; hands are clasped
In joy unspeakable; the mother's arms
Again are folded round the child she loved
And lost. Old sorrows are forgotten now,
Or but remembered to make sweet the hour
That overpays them; wounded hearts that bled
Or broke are healed forever. In the room
Of this grief-shadowed present, there shall be
A present in whose reign no grief shall gnaw
The heart, and never shall a tender tie
Be broken; in whose reign the Eternal Change
That waits on growth and action shall proceed
With everlasting Concord hand in hand."

Victor Hugo, after threescore and ten years of life, in the ripeness and maturity of his splendid genius, thus proclaims the moral necessity of immortality:

"What is it which alleviates and which sanctifies

toil, which renders men strong, wise, patient, just, at once humble and aspiring, but the perpetual vision of a better world, whose light shines through the darkness of the present life? For myself, I believe profoundly in that better world; and, after many struggles, much study, and numberless trials, this is the supreme conviction of my reason, as it is the supreme consolation of my soul."

Hear him speak again at a time when he was rejoicing in the fullness of all his powers:

"I feel in myself the future life. I am like a forest once cut down. The new shoots are stronger and livelier than ever. I am rising, I know, toward the sky. The sunshine is on my head. The earth gives me its generous sap, but heaven lights me with the reflection of unknown worlds. You say the soul is nothing but the resultant of bodily powers. Why, then, is my soul more luminous when my bodily powers begin to fail? Winter is on my head, but eternal spring is in my heart. There I breathe at this hour the fragrance of the lilacs, the violets, and the roses, as at twenty years. The nearer I approach the end, the plainer I hear around me the immortal symphonies of the worlds which invite me. It is marvelous, yet simple. It is a fairy tale, and it is history. For half a century I have been writing my thoughts in prose and verse, history, philosophy, drama, romance, tradition, satire, ode, and song—I have tried all. But I feel I have not said the thousandth part of what is in me. When

I go down to the grave, I can say, like so many others, 'I have finished my day's work,' but I cannot say, 'I have finished my life.' My day's work will begin again the next morning. The tomb is not a blind alley; it is a thoroughfare. It closes on the twilight to open with the dawn."

3. The Christian doctrine of a future life is most rational, most satisfying, most certain in the soul's purest, noblest, most unselfish, most unworldly hours; while it is dim, shadowy, uncertain, unreal when we are disloyal, disobedient, selfish, worldly, and impure. There is a Garden of Eden in every man's life, and in that garden stands the tree of the knowledge of good and evil. The tempter whispers to us that we shall not die if we eat the fruit, but that we shall become as gods; strong, wise, and powerful. Every man listens to that voice, and at some time or other every man hearkens to it, but, instead of the promised increase of knowledge, disobedience is followed by blindness, confusion, and sorrow. To drop the figure, in this life we all have experiences of evil. We are disloyal to the highest right we know. We do not always obey the faithful and friendly monitions of conscience. We are at times grossly selfish. We become worldly, secular-minded, sacrificing principle to policy, right to expediency. Now, if you will take care to analyze your moral state after you have done wrong; when you have been insincere, selfish, envious, grasping, merciless, prayerless; when you have given the reins to the lower and baser nature;

when you have endeavored to stifle the voice of conscience—if, after passing through such experiences, you will question yourself as to the soul's immortality, that great and precious truth will seem to you shadowy, dim, uncertain. It is a statement that every man may verify in his own experience, that wrong-doing, evil dispositions and habits, weaken the force of the evidence for the future life of the soul. A man's moral state often determines whether he is pervious or impervious to the truth.

We are the subjects of goodness, however, as well as of evil. We do not always obey the voice of the insidious tempter. We are capable of resisting, and we do often actually resist and conquer temptation. We have dared to do right sometimes in the face of tremendous odds. We have indignantly trampled beneath our feet the seductive bait of evil. We have compelled our lower nature to serve our higher nature. We have attently listened for the commands of conscience, and, hearing, we have instantly and gladly obeyed. We have been merciful when we were tempted to strike, and when our victim was in our power. We have been patient under the most severe provocation. We have deliberately yielded our cherished desires and plans, to serve and bless others when they were incapable of fully appreciating the sacrifices we were making in their behalf. After all such experiences immortality seemed to be the natural destiny of the soul. We felt within us the beginnings of that eternal life of which Christ spoke. Clear, strong, certain, satisfying, seemed to be the evidences of the soul's supremacy over death. The bare suggestion of annihilation sent an icy shudder through the soul. We recoiled at the thought of it. We felt ourselves to be allied to God and the invisible world by an imperishable bond. Nothing could shake our faith in the soul's celestial and spiritual destiny. Goodness, purity, loyalty of soul, is the unfailing condition of apprehending the highest spiritual and religious truth.

The question arises, in view of these facts, shall we take the verdict of our higher or of our lower natures? Shall we take counsel of that which is good or of that which is evil in us? Shall we learn from that which is best or from that which is worst in us? If we accept the verdict of our highest, finest, noblest faculties, we must accept, and we will accept, the Christian doctrine of a future life. They bring no uncertain, hesitating report on this subject. Distinctly and emphatically do they confirm the teaching of revelation that there is for us an inheritance incorruptible, undefiled, and that fadeth not away. It cannot be possible that our highest and best faculties were made on purpose to deceive us. Then our whole nature is a lie, and God himself is found untrue. If the moral and spiritual powers in us were constructed to mislead and lie to us we are in a bewildering maze, and there is no solid ground upon which we may plant our feet. Truth is clean gone forever, and we are in an endless labyrinth of error. Our moral and spiritual powers must, therefore, be reliable and trustworthy, and they, at their best estate, in explicit and solemn language, declare that man is destined to rise to a glorious immortality.

A man is out on the mountains in a black, stormy night. The rain pours in torrents. He cannot see six inches ahead of him. He is a stranger, and has never traveled the road before, A single false step and he may be dashed down a precipice of five hundred feet. But ever and anon there are broad, vivid sheets of lightning, and they reveal to him the direction of the narrow, winding mountain road. What if he should shut his eyes when the lightning flashes? He would surely lose his way and be dashed to pieces on the rocks below. In the dark and troublous and perplexing ways of this life, God, by the supremacy of our moral natures, gives us light and direction. Let us thankfully accept and loyally follow this light. It will lead us safely through all the devious paths of this mortal pilgrimage, and finally conduct us to the celestial city.

THE REASONABLENESS OF IMMORTALITY.

II.

If a man die, shall he live again?—Job xiv, 14.

WE are considering the reasonableness of the Christian doctrine of a future life. The Christian does not rest his hope of survival ofter death upon the mere suggestions of nature and reason. These suggestions may serve to confirm that hope, but they do not in the first instance produce it. We believe in the future life of the soul, because Jesus Christ, who came out from God, bringing with him the secrets of eternity, revealed to us the great truth that the gift of God is eternal life. He abolished death, and brought life and immortality to light. Because he lives, we shall live also.

It may, however, in an age of doubts and questionings, become the duty of the Christian apologist to show that this doctrine is in nowise repugnant to reason, or contradictory of the facts of man's manifold being. My purpose, then, is not to attempt to prove that the soul is immortal, but to show that the Christian doctrine of immortality is reasonable, and not to be rejected as unworthy of belief on any *a priori* grounds.

1. The belief in immortality is reasonable in the light of the nature and powers of man. Practical scientific men are accustomed to reproach Christian thinkers for lightly esteeming man's physical nature, for failing to recognize and obey the laws of man's physical constitution. The one-sidedness of the Christian is in this respect fully matched by the one-sidedness of the practical scientist. He is disposed to spend all his time and exert all his energies in the study of man's physical organism. If you read Dr. Carpenter on the brain you will feel for the hour that man is nothing but a retort, into which various chemical elements are mingled and by certain physical processes converted into cerebral matter. This cerebral matter, in turn, by some occult and inexplicable process, manufactures thought, emotion, volition, orations, histories, essays, poetry, and scientific treatises. But surely there is something else of man besides muscles, and nerves, and bones, and tendons, and sinews, and ligaments, and veins, and arteries, and cerebral matter. Man does something else than eat, and drink, and digest, and assimilate, and walk, and breathe, and talk, and perform various physical processes. "There is a spirit in man, and the inspiration of the Almighty giveth him understanding." He observes, he perceives, he reflects, he compares, he reasons, he generalizes, he invents, he creates, he conceives, he imagines, he remembers, he is the subject of a large number of purely intellectual processes. Nor have you exhausted

the catalogue of his powers when you have enumerated and analyzed his intellectual faculties. He has emotions, desires, affections, yearnings, aspirations. He loves and he hates, he is sad and he is glad, mighty tides of emotion sometimes convulse, sometime clarify and uplift, his being; he has a sense of the beautiful, of the grand, of the sublime; above all, he possesses the power to perceive moral qualities in actions and to feel the obligatoriness of duty. Physiology is a noble study, but it does not exhaust the knowledge of man. In the name of science, as well as of reason and religion, we must demand psychology as the complement of physiology. No philosophy of man can be constructed which does not include all the facts and powers of his nature.

Consider some of the more noble and spiritually prophetic attributes of man's nature. We speak of man as being capable of goodness, wisdom, justice, truth, love, and holiness. It is an indisputable fact that these qualities do actually belong to man. Man is capable of goodness, he is capable of justice, he is capable of truth, he is capable of love. He knows in some proper sense what justice is, and he can himself pursue such a course of conduct as to entitle him to be described as a just man, or a man of justice. He knows what holiness is, and he is capable of becoming, in a certain sense, holy, so that he may truthfully be described as a holy man. But these qualities, or attributes, are very high, significant, and noble ones. They are the qualities and attributes which we ascribe to the Supreme Being. We speak of God as good, as pure, as holy, as just, as true. Justice, holiness, rectitude, love, purity—these are the moral attributes of God. It is true, they exist in him in infinite amplitude, scope, power, and richness, far transcending all our present power of thought and conception. But justice in God can only be a glorified and infinite form of the justice which we find in man. It differs in degree; it cannot differ in kind. If justice in the Divine Being is something other and different in kind, in quality, in essence, from justice in man, then man does not really know what justice is, for it is only by the germ of justice in his own breast that he can interpret justice in God. There are not two kinds of justice—human justice and divine justice. Justice is a quality of moral conduct, and in its essential nature and disposition must be the same every-where. In one nature it may be feeble, imperfect, varying, in another strong, steady, constant, in still another infinite and unsearchable, but still it is justice. Justice in man, therefore, is, in germ form, the same justice that in glowing and glorious perfection resides in the heart of God. Love in man is a true type of love in God. With us love may be but as a drop of water, with God it is a mighty ocean; but it is love alike in his and the human heart.

Man, then, is now actually possessed of GOD-LIKE powers, qualities, dispositions, and attributes. He does actually partake of the divine nature.

He is allied to God by identity of moral capacity. His nature is high, noble, spiritual, prophetic of divinity. Now, if man with these powers be mortal and perishable, if with such capacities death shall utterly annihilate him, he is surely a waste of creative power; he has been far too highly equipped for his miserable destiny. Why load the ship with such a precious cargo, if it be known beforehand that it must be wrecked, and every thing be lost? Why endow man with the capacities and powers of a god, and then give him the destiny of the worm? In the language of the great Robert Hall, "man, considered apart from his immortality, is the vainest thing under the sun." The white elephants of India are said to attain the age of a hundred years. The average age of man is thirty-three years. If the elephant with his powers is given a life of a century, and the man with his powers but the third of a century, creation is more than a mystery—it is a horrible imposture, a cruel lie. There are oak-trees in England twelve centuries old. They were there when Harold fell at Hastings, and William the Conqueror introduced the Normans. Through all the vicissitudes and glories of English history they have stood as silent remembrancers of the past. Thirty-six generations of children have laughed and played beneath their wide-spreading boughs. In the meantime, what a galaxy of illustrious names has arisen in the English firmament. What a noble host of geniuses has been reared on British soil. Chaucer, and Spenser, and

Shakespeare, and Milton, and Locke, and Newton, and Burke, and Chatham, and Macaulay; Latimer, Ridley, Hampden, Barrow, Baxter, Jeremy Taylor, and Wesley—names that stir our sluggish blood and rouse us once more to high emprise of thought and deed—these all have come and gone. The quick, cruel, and rapacious grave has swallowed them forever from human sight. If death ends all, if extinction was the sad destiny of these choice and gifted spirits, then English oaks have a grander sweep of being than English men. How anomalous and shocking and abortive the creation that lengthens out through twelve centuries the life of an insensate, unthinking tree, and, becoming impatient of the splendid genius of the thinking Shakespeare, stamps out his life in fifty years! It is to such monstrous suppositions that the denial of the soul's immortality reduces us. A being like man, capable of participating in the divine life, possessed of qualities directly allying him to the invisible and intelligent Creator—such a being, I affirm, is not to have the destiny of the worm.

Henry Thomas Buckle founded his belief in immortality on one single capacity of man's nature; namely, his power to love. Here is his statement of the argument:

"Look now at the way in which this godlike and fundamental principle (the love principle) of our nature acts. As long as we are with those whom we love, and as long as the sense of security is unimpaired, we rejoice, and the remote consequences of our love are usually forgotten. Its fears and its risks are unheeded. But when the dark day approaches, and the moment of sorrow is at hand, other and yet essential parts of our affection come into play. And if, perchance, the struggle has been long and arduous; if we have been tempted to cling to hope when hope should have been abandoned, so much the more are we at the last changed and humbled. To note the slow but inevitable march of disease, to watch the enemy stealing in at the gate, to see the strength gradually waning, the limbs tottering more and more, the noble faculties dwindling by degrees, the eye paling and losing its luster, the tongue faltering as it vainly tries to utter its words of endearment, the very lips hardly able to smile with their wonted tenderness—to see this is hard indeed to bear, and many of the strongest natures have sunk under it. But when even this is gone, when the very signs of life are mute, when the last faint tie is severed, and there lies before us naught save the shell and husk of what we loved too well, then truly, if we believed the separation were final, how could we stand up and live? We have staked all upon a single cast, and lost the stake. There, where we have garnered up our hearts, and where our treasure is, thieves break in and spoil. Methinks that in that moment of desolation the best of us would succumb but for the deep conviction that all is not really over, that we have as yet only seen a part, and that something remains behind; something behind — something which the eye of reason cannot discern, but on which the eye of affection is fixed. What is that which, passing over us like a shadow, strains the aching vision as we gaze at it? Whence comes that sense of mysterious companionship in the midst of solitude, that ineffable feeling which cheers the afflicted? Why is it that, at these times, our minds are thrown back on themselves, and, being so thrown, have a forecast of another and a higher state? If this be a delusion it is one which the affections have themselves created, and we must believe that the purest and noblest elements of our nature conspire to deceive us. . . . It is, then, to that sense of immortality with which the affections inspire us, that I would appeal for the best proof of the reality of a future life."

To the same effect is the following quotation from the brilliant and eloquent pen of the late George D. Prentice: "Men seldom think of the great event of death until the shadow falls across their own pathway, hiding from their eyes the face of loved ones whose loving smile was the sunlight of their existence. Death is the antagonist of life and the cool thought of the tomb is the skeleton of all fears. We do not want to go through the dark valley, although its dark passage may lead to the grave, even with princes for bed-fellows." The same truth, namely, that the human spirit is too rich in its treasures of love ever to be destroyed by death, finds beautiful expression in Talfourd's exquisite drama of *Ion*.

The hope of immortality there so eloquently uttered by the death-devoted Greek finds deep responses in every thoughtful soul. When about to yield his young existence as a sacrifice to fate, his Clemantha asks him if they should ever meet again, to which he replies: "I have asked that dreadful question of the hills that looked eternal, of the clear streams that flow forever, of the stars among whose fields of azure my raised spirit has walked in glory. All were dumb. But when I gaze upon thy living face I feel that there is something in the love that mantles its beauty that cannot wholly perish. We shall meet again, Clemantha."

2. It is an easy and natural transition from these thoughts to the next line of suggestion and argument—that is, that the infinite love of the Author of the universe renders reasonable a serene faith in immortality. Man has more than intellect; he has heart. Richly equipped as he is in purely intellectual faculties, he is even more magnificently endowed in his affectional nature. His knowledge may be partial and fragmentary, his logic faulty, his generalizations hasty, his conclusions inaccurate and unreliable, but his love is immense, significant, divine almost. The power and patience of human affection, especially in woman, is indescribable. A horrible crime is committed in the community. The perpetrator of the foul deed is quickly arrested, tried, convicted, sentenced to execution. The community applauds this swift execution of justice. The day of execution arrives, and in all the crowd

surrounding the doomed man there is not a single relenting, pitying eye. But crouching yonder in the shadow of the scaffold is a gray-haired woman. It is the criminal's mother. She loves him still, nor will she ever cease to love him. At her knee he knelt in childhood. She solaced his early sorrows. He was her hope and her joy. He may be a murderer, the whole community may have risen up against him in righteous indignation, he may have stepped from the scaffold into eternity, but his image is indelibly impressed upon her heart, and her great love is sure to invent some extenuation of his awful crime. The literature of love is not written, save in the Book of God. The love of a mother, of a father, of brother and sister, of wife and husband, of friends, of nature, of beauty, of right, this is the richest, noblest, divinest part of man. All that is good in human history, all that ameliorates, and hallows, and sanctifies the life of to-day, all that presages the final emancipation of humanity from the slavery of ignorance, of sin, and of hate, is an outgrowth and development of pure and holy love.

All the love that manifests itself in human hearts is simply the overflow of the love of the divine Heart. This human love must have a fountain somewhere, it must have a source. It springs from the inexhaustible depths of the divine nature. Love in man, the effect, argues love in God, the cause. Love in the being produced necessitates love in the being producing. The love that beautifies, ennobles, and spiritualizes our life had its origin in the immeasurable tides of love that perpetually flow in the ocean of the divine nature. Love in God, like every other quality, has a grandeur, a scope, a power, far beyond the measure of our thought. He is infinite; so is his love, so is his justice, so is his wisdom, so is his holiness.

In this infinite and almighty love of God, resides the sure hope of immortality. Human love seeks the highest welfare of its objects. The purer, the holier, the more unselfish a mother's love, the more hopefully, patiently and continuously does she seek the highest good of her children. Love in man is imperfect; in God it is perfect. In man it is narrow; in God it is boundless. In man it is often unwise and capricious; in God it is always just and wise. If an intelligent and pure human love seeks the highest welfare of the beloved object, will not the infinitely pure and intelligent love of God seek the highest welfare of his children? What is our highest welfare: extinction, or immortal life? There is but one answer to that question. The highest welfare of man demands immortality; another and a higher sphere of being, in which all his faculties shall have a full fruition and a perfect culture. If the strong and unwasting love of God is not a dream and a fiction, the soul shall have such a destiny.

Let us bring these separate lights together, and behold how doubt, and fear, and darkness flee away. The reasonableness of the Christian doctrine of a future life is seen in the light of the two scientific doctrines of the indestructibility of matter and the conservation of energy; for if matter and force be imperishable, why not mind? It is seen in the luminous and creative hours of intellectual and moral life, hours in which the soul seems to take wings and fly far above the noise, and strife, and tumult of time; it is seen in the prophetic intimations of conscience, pointing onward to a future state of righteous retribution; it is seen in the universality of the belief in a future life among both civilized and savage men, in ancient and modern times; it is seen in the longings of the noblest natures after a more congenial culture and a more consummate perfection; it is seen in the increased fervor with which men desire immortality as they become more highly and finely developed; it is seen in the satisfaction and certainty with which the soul regards a future life in its purest, most unselfish, and most unworldly hours; it is seen in the glory, and magnificence, and spirituality of the attributes of man's nature; above all, it is seen in the infinite love of the intelligent Author of the universe—a love strong, wise, and patient enough to rescue us from extinction not only, but to enthrone us with the principalities, and powers, and dominions of the heavenly places.

Ten or twelve years ago, when spending a summer in the mountains of West Virginia, I enjoyed, in company with a warmly appreciative friend, since a devoted missionary of our Church in India, the most glorious sunset of my life. One moment the light, fleecy, snow-like clouds seemed to be resting on the tops of the trees on the distant mountains, and then again they were all aflame with the reflected glories of the fast-sinking sun, shining like a ball of burnished gold, fresh from the hand of God. As we stood there together, silently drinking in the solemn inspiration of the scene, the sun went down, *but not out.* Its light dawned upon another hemisphere. Our horizon was necessarily a narrow, circumscribed one, and hence it seemed to us as though it had disappeared forever. As God and the angels saw it, it poured its grateful flood of light and heat on the other half of the globe. It was night with us; it was day-dawn with them. So is it with the pure souls we have loved. There is sometimes a solemn beauty in their dying, which may be likened to the lingering glories of the setting sun. Owing to our narrow intellectual and moral horizon, it may appear to us that the light and love of these souls have been quenched forever. Not so. They just begin to live. It is night with us; it is day-dawn with them. They rise into the Eternal Presence, they rejoice in the beatific vision, they are enfranchised forever with all the dignities, privileges, and immunities of the skies.

"There are no dead.
'Tis true, many of them are gone;
Singly they came, singly they departed;
When their work was done, they lay down to sleep—
But never one hath *died;*
Forms may change, but spirit is immortal."

THE CHRISTIAN HEAVEN.

And God shall wipe away all tears from their eyes; and there shall be no more death, neither sorrow, nor crying, neither shall there be any more pain; for the former things are passed away.— Rev. 21. 24.

And there shall be no more curse: but the throne of God and of the Lamb shall be in it; and his servants shall serve him· and they shall see his face; and his name shall be in their foreheads.— Rev. 22. 3, 4.

NEXT to the great truth of the existence of God, and the moral character of God, the fundamental and far-reaching teaching of the Christian religion is that there is a future immortal life for holy souls. In all its generations, in all its struggles, in all its sins, and in all its sorrows, the human race has been supported and directed by the vast, solemn, glowing hope that goodness and purity, love and duty, are not born to die; that they shall survive the dreaded catastrophe of death, and emerge in great power and splendor in the eternal world. As from the overhanging clouds come the grateful showers that refresh and revive the parched earth, so from this hope, of a supreme, ample, and perfect life beyond, come all the glorious influences and inspirations that quicken and strengthen men amid the wastes and losses, the pain and struggles, of the life that now is. One of the soul's native and ineradicable beliefs is that "earth has no sorrow that heaven cannot heal." We feel instinctively that under the reign of a perfectly righteous God, to whose power there are no ascertainable limits, justice must finally be done. We know that justice is not always completely done so far as the experiences, purposes, and issues of this present life are concerned; and to a moral mind the conclusion is short, sharp, and irresistible, that there is another and higher life where the ways of God will be manifested as the ways of love, equity, and truth.

This expectation of heaven has been universal. The poor Indian, whose mind had not been tutored by science or literature, aspired to a humble heaven where his faithful dog should bear him company. The ancient Greek had his fair Elysian fields and his bright islands of the blest. The rude Scandinavian dreamed of a green paradise amid the wastes. The mystic and contemplative Hindoo yearns after the deep peace and unbroken rest of the Nirvana. All nations have pictured to themselves beyond the grave, according to the order of their own genius, some

> "Island valley of Avilion,
> Where falls not hail or rain, or any snow,
> Nor ever wind blows loudly."

The text suggests for our theme the Christian heaven. First, the Christian revelation of heaven is remarkable for its silent suggestiveness, its wise reticence, its noble concealment and reserve. "It doth not yet appear what we shall be," ought to be the motto of all who seek to study and understand the really Christian revelation of heaven. What we are *not* taught in the Scriptures concerning the life of the blessed hereafter is quite as significant, quite as luring to the imagination, and quite as prophetic to the soul, as what is made known to us. Many questions may be started about heaven to which the Scriptures furnish no clear, decisive, or adequate reply. Where is heaven? And there is no answer in the Bible of the Christian. What is heaven? And there is no answer. What organizations, if any, do spirits have? And there is no definite answer. What are the employments, the disciplines, the studies, the activities, the various spiritual gymnasia of heaven? There is no answer. What is the mode of the life of departed spirits? What means of locomotion are theirs? How do they acquire knowledge? By observation, perception, study, reflection, and reasoning, or by the quick flash of unerring intuition, by swift, piercing insight? Are the relationships of earth carried on beyond? What is the meaning of such words as these: " In heaven they neither marry nor are given in marriage, but all are as the angels of God?" Does the child remain a child? And many a mother yearns for an answer. Do varieties of temperament still obtain? Is truth over yonder cut into so many regulation blocks, all alike, or is it as we find it here, touched, colored, modified, by various experiences, temperaments, and dispositions? These and many like questions are unanswered in the Christian revelation of heaven. Much is told us, but much is left for the free play of our faculty, for the wistful yearning of the imagination; much is left for the joyous surprise of actual discovery when we enter upon its high and glorious fruitions.

We will each one of us find something in heaven which we do not expect. There is that about the disclosure of heaven in the New Testament which we find in the character of some men and women—namely, a noble reticence, a quiet, significant, attractive reserve. I do not like people that are shallow; I do not like people who are as shallow as meadow pools that children can bale out in an afternoon at play; I do not like people who, after you have seen them two or three times, you know all there is to them and in them, and you can tell precisely what kind of a life they have lived. I like to meet men and women that are deep and reticent, and are always suggesting to me how great they might be under other circumstances; how they would suffer and be strong, what they might do in emergencies, and through what emergencies they may have passed. I like to meet people that are reserved occasionally. And I am glad that there is enough in heaven to perpetually lure us, and draw us forth, and charm us. Such reticences never cease to interest us, we are perpetually drawn toward them.

It is better for us, doubtless, that heaven is thus left surrounded by a tender and vague mystery. If a full and immediate revelation were made to us, I have no doubt that we would become dissatisfied with our present world and life, and our present mode of discipline. We would abandon, or, at least, neglect, the work God has given us to do. The effect on children of the anticipation of some great joy varies. Have you ever studied it? Have you ever opened out the contents of a joy to the child? If you fix a day for it, it will not study much; it likes to count up the time; it enjoys waiting and seeing how long it will be, and running and asking questions; but it does not study much. But you leave it vague, indefinite, undefined; you tell a child that *if* it studies well, some great, rich joy will be given it, and never tell what the contents of that joy are, or when the day will come that shall unfold it, and it will study. So is it with us; if all the contents of heaven should be revealed to us we would be very listless, we would be asking questions all the time, we would neglect the work we are now given to do, we would be always wishing for that higher life to be given us, for I take it that, as God and the angels see us, we are about as foolish a family of children as could well be imagined.

As it is, ample room is left for the free exercise of the imagination and of the affections. More than that: the canvas is furnished us; the pigment, the palette, and the brush are given us, and we can paint each his own picture of that fair and radiant world, always remembering that the reality will far surpass our noblest hopes, our most delicate fancies, our finest conceptions, our most gorgeous creations. When once we see heaven, we will be willing that all our pictures of heaven shall fade and die.

Second, Heaven, as it is disclosed to us in the word of God, is free from all elements and sources of disturbance, disquiet, pain, struggle, and sin.

This life is a life of growth, a life of development by growth, and, therefore, necessarily a life of disturbance, of disquietude, of imperfections, of pain-bearing elements. All these are excluded from heaven. Did you ever take your Bible, especially the New Testament, and try to think about heaven, and find out how many "nos" and "nots" are used to describe it? There are a great many of them. There shall be "no night in heaven;" there shall be "no sun or moon;" there shall be "no more curse;" there shall be "no abominations;" there shall be "no more hunger or thirst;" there shall be "no sorrow;" there shall be no crying;" there shall be "no more pain;" there shall be "no more death." "The former things are *all* passed away."

Consider now some of the disturbing elements that will be absent from the heavenly life. All that we mean by ignorance—and we mean a great deal by it—will not be in heaven. There will be growth, elevation, development there, but no ignorance that costs, no ignorance that wastes. There will be no poverty there. Disease—alas! what disturbances and inquietude that causes here; pain—that vast, undiscovered mystery; sorrow of the heart—how much there is of it in this world; suffering of the mind, struggle, loneliness, temptation, and, waiting for us all, yonder in ambush, death! Now, if all these elements of evil, all these elements of pain, all these elements of perturbation were taken out of this world, what a different world it would be! I see I wrote here in pencil, in looking over these notes before coming in, " What a glorious world it would be with no ignorance, no poverty, no disease, no pain, no sorrow of heart, no suffering of the mind, no temptation, no death!" This is a radiantly beautiful world God has made for us, my friends. What skies there are over our heads; what glorious star-lit nights; what green fields are on the face of the earth; what mighty seas; what fragrant flowers; what singing birds! O what a world this would be without ignorance, or poverty, or disease, or pain, or temptation, or heart-sorrow, or mind-anguish, or the chilling dread of death! Do we realize all that is involved in a life free from these elements? Have you ever, weary of strife, discouraged with yourself, discouraged with others, —have you ever closed your eyes and repeated over and over again, until sweet peace came, these words: " For the former things are passed away, for the former things are passed away, for the former things are passed away?"

The revealed positive elements of the heavenly life combine to make it eminently spiritual, rational, and attractive, and to crown it with ineffable honor and glory. Purity is the first distinctive heritage of those who enter this heavenly life. The purity of heaven may be described in two ways: First, negatively. So it is described to us in the word of God: " There shall in no wise enter into it any thing that defileth, neither whatsoever worketh abomination or maketh a lie!" But there is another short sentence, very significant: "Without are dogs." Have you ever read an Oriental traveler's account of what this sentence means; of how many dogs they have in these crowded cities of the Orient, and of how, for safety and cleanliness and health, at night all the dogs are left outside of the gate of the city? "Without are dogs." But it is given to us positively: "After this I beheld, and, lo, a great multitude, which no man could number, of all nations, and kindreds, and people, and tongues, stood before the throne, and before the Lamb, clothed with white robes, and palms in their hands; and cried with a loud voice, saying, Salvation to our God which sitteth upon the throne, and unto the Lamb." We know little of purity here, little either of its real nature, or of its perfection, or of its power, or of its final fruits, but we know enough to know that purity is heaven. There we shall be pure without fault, without spot, without pain, and, what is better, without peril. It is a fine and a deep saying of Confucius, the Chinese sage, that "Heaven means principle."

Another positive element in the life of heaven is triumphant joy in worship. We read often in the Revelation of John of great voices in heaven, and never are they so great or so many as when the joys of the redeemed are described. "And a voice came out of the throne, saying, Praise our God, all ye his servants, and ye that fear him, both small and great. And I heard as it were the voice of a great multitude, and as the voice of many waters, and as the voice of mighty thunderings, saying, Alleluia: for the Lord God omnipotent reigneth." I take it that they must have something like congregational singing in heaven! In the fifteenth chapter of Revelation, second and third verses, we read as follows: " And I saw as it were a sea of glass mingled with fire: and them that had gotten the victory over the beast, and over his image, and over his mark, and over the number of his name, stand on the sea of glass, having the harps of God. And they sing the song of Moses the servant of God, and the song of the Lamb, saying, Great and marvelous are thy works, Lord God Almighty; just and true are thy ways, thou King of saints." And here is the most magnificent description of singing, or joy in worship in heaven, to be found within the lids of the great book: "And I beheld, and, lo, in the midst of the throne and of the four beasts, and in the midst of the elders, stood a Lamb as it had been slain, having seven horns and seven eyes, which are the seven Spirits of God sent forth into all the earth. And he came and took the book out of the right hand of him that sat upon the throne. And when he had taken the book, the four beasts and four and twenty elders fell down before the Lamb, having every one of them harps, and golden vials full of odor, which are the prayers of saints. And they sung a new song, saying, Thou art worthy to take the book, and to open the seals thereof:

for thou wast slain, and hast redeemed us to God by thy blood out of every kindred, and tongue, and people, and nation; and hast made us unto our God kings and priests: and we shall reign on the earth. And I beheld, and I heard the voice of many angels round about the throne, and the beasts, and the elders: and the number of them was ten thousand times ten thousand, and thousands of thousands; saying with a loud voice, Worthy is the Lamb that was slain to receive power, and riches, and wisdom, and strength, and honor, and glory, and blessing. And every creature which is in heaven, and on the earth, and under the earth, and such as are in the sea, and all that are in them, heard I saying, Blessing, and honor, and glory, and power, be unto him that sitteth upon the throne, and unto the Lamb forever and forever."

These are mere glimpses, intimations, tokens, poetic symbols of heaven, but they are such glowing poetic symbols of heaven as would have delighted the imaginations of Shakespeare or of Milton. They describe the mighty joy of the redeemed, enfranchised, empowered and worshiping spirits of heaven. We were made for joy. We were made for the highest joy, and the highest joy springs from the spontaneous exercise of our highest faculties. The keen delight and rapture that we feel in the presence of something great, vast, sublime, is, I suppose, nearly akin to the feeling that we must have in heaven, not once, but perpetually. Jean Paul Richter says that it is the office of music to dilate our souls to their full capacity for the infinite. I shall never forget the first time I saw the sea, landsman as I was; being brought up in a portion of the country where they even did not have a river. When in July, 1877, about seven o'clock in the evening, I gazed for the first time upon the waste of waters on the coast of Massachusetts, my heart was dilated to its full capacity for the infinite. I almost forgot the house to which I was going, and I was indifferent to whether I ever reached it. I did not sleep at all that night. I am glad I did not; I am glad I was young enough, foolish enough, enthusiastic enough, sentimental enough, to lie awake all night and listen to the moan and murmur of the mighty sea. I am glad that I hunted all the poets through, and re-read with a fresh joy all they had ever said about the sea. I am glad that I seemed almost to have no special use for the gross earth for a day or two. I never stepped more light and free. I take it that there are oceans and mountains, or those things which in our growth will fulfill the functions or offices of oceans, and mountains, and Niagaras, in heaven. If God could make a few on this earth, for our present growth and joy, he can make a great many for our everlasting growth in heaven.

The life of heaven is dignified by noble and exalted service. The heavenly life is not to be one of inglorious ease or of rapt contemplation. We know not the nature or the manifoldness of the activities of the upper world, but we do know that high and holy service shall be appointed us. " Therefore are they before the throne, and *serve* him day and night in his temple; and he that sitteth on the throne shall dwell among them." "And there shall be no more curse, but the throne of God and of the Lamb shall be in it, and his *servants* shall *serve* him."

These passages teach that we are to have work in heaven; that we are not to be aristocratic loungers there, like the sons of an entailed nobility. They are mistaken who suppose that the heavenly world is one of idle dreaminess and delicious languor. This work is to be unselfish. You know here we all work centripetally; we like to work so as to have every thing run toward ourselves. There the Book says we shall serve HIM. The blessedness of all work is to be found in the extinction of self. Our work there is to be done amid associations and surroundings of the highest order and of the noblest character. "Before the throne;" "In his temple;" "He that sitteth on the throne shall dwell among them." This work is to be constant, tireless, and unfatiguing. "They serve him day and night;" "There is no night there." They never need to rest, and that is the reason they have no night. Here we become weary, fatigued, exhausted. We need to go in the repair shop at least eight hours out of every twenty-four. Here we mix foreign and corrosive elements with our work, as fear, envy, ambition, worry, anxiety, apprehensiveness. We never do our best work when we are depressed by fear, cankered with anxiety, corroded by envy, narrowed or dwarfed with the secular and worldly spirit. We do our best work when we are free from all these things. Have you ever gone into a great machine shop, with a handful of small steel filings, and when not observed dropped a few of them on any wheel? If so, no matter how large the wheel, or how rapid in its revolution, there was a creaking, gritting, grating sound, that betokened a sharp friction, no matter how small the particles may have been. There will be no steel filings on the wheels of our industry over there! We will work without fear; we will work without envy; we will work without anxiety; we will work without fretting; we will work without malice; we will work without wishing to push out and crowd down the man who stands next to us in the ranks of life.

The crowning glory of heaven is the open vision of God. All Scripture teaching concerning the future life takes its prevailing color, is toned and determined by the thought that at last we shall see God. Job comforts and strengthens himself by this thought amid the darkness and pain and suffering of which he was the struggling and bewildered victim: "Whom I shall see for myself, and mine eyes shall behold, and not another." So the Psalmist: "As for me, I will behold thy face in righteousness: I will be satisfied when I awake in thy likeness." The prophet Isaiah, in speaking of the secure and satisfying heritage of the righteous, says that "bread shall be given him; his waters shall be sure. Thine eyes shall see the King in his beauty: they shall behold the land that is very far off." "And they shall see his face, and his name shall be in their foreheads."

The yearning to see God, the longing and passionate desire to behold the face of our Father, is the deepest and strongest and most abiding of human hearts and human lives. "O Lord, I beseech thee, show me thy glory," was the passionate prayer of Moses. "Whom have I in heaven but thee? and there is none on earth whom I desire beside thee." "As the hart panteth after the waterbrooks, so panteth my soul after thee, O God. My soul thirsteth for God, for the living God: when shall I come and appear before God?" So Job cried in the midst of his utter desolation and sharp agony: "O that I knew where I might find him! that I might come even to his seat! I would order my cause before him, and fill my mouth with arguments."

This is the crown and summit of heaven's glory: that we shall see his face, and that his name shall be written in our foreheads. Whatever we seek, we shall find it all in God—knowledge, forgiveness, purity, light, love, inspiration, and work.

My friends, the years do not lag; they are not heavy-footed; they are hurrying us onward, homeward, and heavenward. God is surely bringing us to himself, though not by paths of our own ordering, not by ways of our own choosing. Sometimes by the radiant, glorious, sun-lit mount; sometimes by the damp, chill, mist-covered valley; sometimes by flowery vales and green fields, amid the babbling of cooling water-brooks; sometimes in a dry and thirsty land where no water is; but still it is not the hand of a stranger, it is our Father's hand that leads us home. We walk with doubting, uncertain, unsteady feet, we slip and fall, we wander from the way, and are like lost sheep upon the mountains; we sin, and suffer, and repent, and sin again. "Mercy would long ago have been wearied out if mercy were a human thing," but still we hope and still we are safe, because the eternal God is our refuge, and underneath us are the everlasting arms.

> "My feet are worn and weary with the march
>   Over the rough road and up the steep hill-side;
> O city of our God, I fain would see
>   Thy pastures green, where peaceful waters glide!
>
> "My eyes are weary looking at the sin,
>   Impiety, and scorn upon the earth;
> O city of our God, within thy walls
>   All—all are clothed again with thy new birth.
>
> "My heart is weary of its own deep sin—
>   Sinning, repenting, sinning still again;
> When shall my soul thy glorious presence feel,
>   And find, dear Saviour, it is free from stain?
>
> "Patience, poor soul! the Saviour's feet were worn,
>   The Saviour's heart and head were weary too;
> His garments stained and travel-worn and old,
>   His vision blinded with a pitying dew.
>
> "Love thou the path of sorrows that he trod;
>   Toil on, and wait in patience for thy rest;
> O city of our God! we soon shall see
>   Thy glorious walls—home of the loved and blest."

THE END.

www.ingramcontent.com/pod-product-compliance
Lightning Source LLC
Chambersburg PA
CBHW022051230426
43672CB00008B/1143